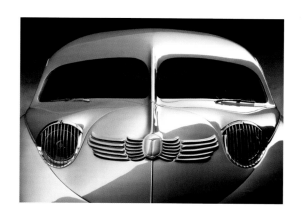

MOTORCARS
of the CLASSIC ERA

MICHAEL FURMAN

Harry N. Abrams, Inc. Publishers

A TEHABI BOOK

1934 Voisin C15 ets Saliot Roadster

For my children

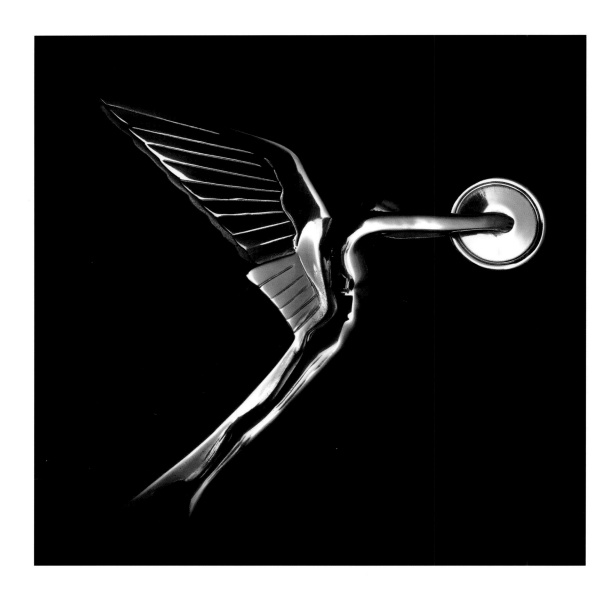

Hood Ornament
1930 Isotta-Fraschini Model 8-A
by Castagna

TABLE OF CONTENTS

Front Detail
1925 Voisin C3L Berline Transformable
by J. Rothschild & Son

INTRODUCTION

The automobile has become the definitive industrial and artistic expression of the modern age. With beautiful sweeping lines, elegant details, and dramatic colors, it expresses the tastes and trends of an industrial society—one that is moving toward the future with respect for the past.

Automobiles occupy a unique place in our culture. They allow us freedom of movement, a lifestyle we otherwise might not enjoy. More than just a means of transportation, they make an emotional statement. We use motorcars to see the world and to be seen by it. In a sense, we allow automobiles to define who we are—to tell the world of our successes, even our excesses.

The motorcars of the classic era—1925 through 1948—reflect an extraordinary segment of world history. It was a time of tremendous contrasts, from fabulous wealth to crushing depression. A time of frightening political turmoil that culminated in World War II and redrew the map of Europe. Yet, throughout all this uncertainty, the automobile flourished. Beautiful coach-built designs by Figoni et Falaschi, Jean Bugatti, Jacques Sautchik, Dutch Darrin, Gordon Buehrig, and many others showed the world what humankind's imagination could muster even though disaster loomed on the horizon. Fanciful concepts—graceful lines, elegant curves, and a palette of sophisticated colors—belied the undercurrents of violence and political change. Craftsmanship was at a premium, with unusual materials—rare woods, exotic hides, state-of-the-art metals, and even Lalique crystal—creating grand statements that have not been made since.

Distinct automotive trends grew from major geographic regions: the United States, Great Britain, and the Continent. In Europe, the automobile belonged only to the privileged; rigid economic and social structures across the Atlantic did not allow the common person such luxury as his or her own personal transportation. But in the United States, Henry Ford gave that freedom to every person with the advent of his assembly-line production. And thus began a vast differentiation in the world's development of the automobile and the lifestyles it produced. America—with its sprawling land and spirit of independence—soon favored larger vehicles and individual transportation. In Europe, however, where automobiles were first created for the elite, cities of confined spaces and narrow roads necessitated smaller cars in conjunction with better rail and metro systems.

However different, each country eventually found its own automotive personality. And while the French Bugatti, Hispano, Delage, and Delahaye led the way, the British Rolls-Royce and Bentley, Italy's Alfa Romeo, Germany's Mercedes-Benz, and the American Duesenberg, Cadillac, and Packard all contributed to this glorious era of automotive design. Each machine became an expression of its country's heritage, artistic influences, industrial capability, and even political intentions.

In Great Britain, the automobile industry still clung to its carriage-building roots, continuing this aesthetic far longer than did the Americans or Europeans. More than anyone, the British worked within a limited range of proportion and subdued colors and never strayed far from conservative solutions. The offering from Sir Frederick Henry Royce and the Honourable Charles Stewart Rolls—the Rolls-Royce—exemplifies that moderate approach even today.

In other countries, the driving force was speed. Mercedes-Benz expressed power: long hoods, intimidating grilles, and massive supercharger pipes. It was a political statement as much as an automotive one and a glimpse of things to come. The Italians embraced athletic performance, too, but then combined it with aesthetic romance. An automobile's look, they believed, had to be as beautiful as its performance. The result: the unforgettable Alfa Romeo racecars of Scuderia Ferrari.

The French took the concept of aesthetics one step further. An object had to be beautiful, period. They held competitions, or *concours d'elegances*, where coach-builders displayed their art. That tradition has continued to this day, as many a Delage, Delahaye, Talbot-Lago, and Voisin, restored to its original splendor, vies for the honor of Best of Show.

One of France's greatest automotive engineers, Ettore Bugatti, was also the world's greatest mechanical artist. Trained as a sculptor—his father a famous artist—Bugatti's designs grew from his love of fine art and his desire to excel at everything he attempted, from locomotive and airplane engines to the greatest racecars of his era. His son Jean Bugatti continued his father's aesthetic legacy, achieving legendary status with the 1938 Bugatti Type 57SC Atlantic Coupé—believed by many to be the most dramatic car in the world, the perfect synthesis of art and engineering.

The French stylists of the golden age were tremendously talented, and they accommodated the custom-built orientation of their clientele. Their inspiration came from unusual places—the power of locomotives, the freedom of flight. Sweeping fenders, for instance, with chrome accents, gave the sense of motion while at rest. And the creations of Figoni et Falaschi were like waves rolling down the highway: fluid yet powerful. At least the automobile had the feel of aerodynamics if not the true benefits.

The automotive heritage of the United States, on the other hand, could not have been more different. In post–World War I America, Ford's Model T reigned supreme. It was inexpensive, relatively small, and lightweight. Produced in enor-mous numbers—fifteen million were made from 1908 to 1927—the Model T was simple transportation for the American masses. And Mr. Ford preferred to paint all of them black! The "Tin Lizzie," as it was dubbed, was fine for the middle classes, but the wealthy wanted more. Grand in size and more dramatic in color, the Packards, Cadillacs, Chryslers, Pierce-Arrows, and Duesenbergs made tremendous statements of superiority both on and off the road.

Yet even these high-end cars still maintained a turn-of-the-century aesthetic. So, in order for the market to move in a more sophisticated direction, the Americans of the 1920s and 1930s looked to European influence. Harley Earl's admiration of the Hispano-Suiza, for instance, was evident in his 1927 LaSalle. And Earl brought extravagant European style to the Art & Colour Section of General Motors, too. With contrasting fenders, beltlines, hoods, trim, and any number of interior and canvas top variations, GM's Cadillacs and LaSalles were available in over four hundred dazzling color combinations. Similarly, in the late 1930s, Dutch Darrin introduced a more stylish aesthetic to the Packard. After working for years in France, he lowered the body, cut down its doors, and made the Packard more dashing for Clark Gable and his other Hollywood clientele.

Errett Lobban Cord, American automotive tycoon and owner of the Auburn Automobile Company, also made his cars to compete with the Continent's best. His Model J Duesenberg was available only as a running chassis, which required the commissioning of a handmade coach-built body—a nod to the custom-made automobiles of Europe. The great coachbuilders of Europe and the United States contributed to the 481 Duesenberg convertibles, sedans, speedsters, coupés, roadsters, and town cars built from 1928 through 1936. The variety was endless. Cord's cross-pollination of American engineering and European design was a success.

Meanwhile, the American automobiles of the post–Depression Era became lower, their windshields raked back. Hoods stretched on forever, but as dual cowls and chauffeurs with driver's compartments became less common, only two people could travel at once. Cars became more mechanically sophisticated and easier to operate, and as a result, more and more owners chose to drive themselves. It appeared less ostentatious, but it was still an expression of power and control.

Some of these new, more elaborate designs worked better in two dimensions while others translated well from paper to metal. Early automobiles, for instance, had a number of separate and sometimes disorganized elements at the front. Radiator shells with mascots dominated, and headlights, driving lights, and fog lights fought for attention with horns and bumpers—all made of chrome. Gordon Buehrig resolved many of these issues in 1935 when he penned two landmark designs: the Auburn 851 Speedster and the Cord 810. Buehrig's designs were elegant and complete—they worked from every angle, balanced and in perfect harmony.

Unfortunately, as the decade progressed it became increasingly difficult for the smaller specialty builders to compete. On the Continent, war was at hand, and economic pressures were growing. One grand marque after another closed its doors or merged with a former competitor to remain in existence. Many of Europe's finest firms were closed for economic reasons, converted to the production of war machinery, or destroyed in the conflict. In the United States, passengercar production completely ceased in 1942 and did not restart until 1946. New designs, new tooling, and new plants had to wait while manufacturers produced prewar designs just to meet the pent-up demand for new cars.

The French builders—Delahaye, Delage, Talbot, and Bugatti—soldiered on for a few years, each one refusing to die, but without the ability to rebuild their factories,

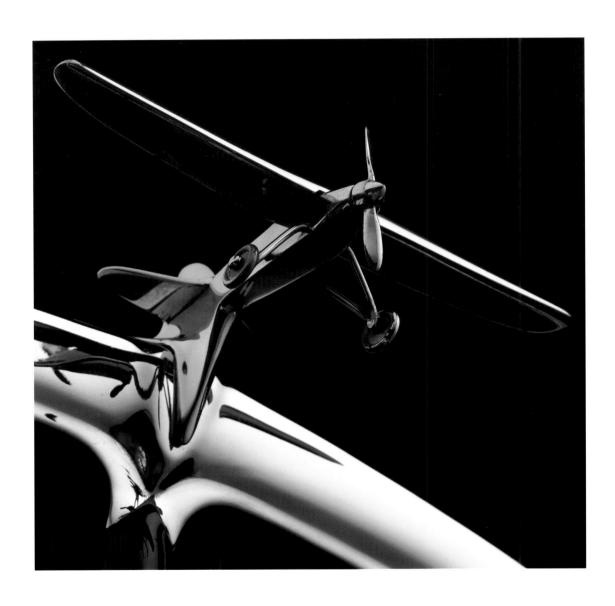

Hood Ornament
1930 Franklin Series 147 Sport Runabout

let alone their past glories. Many of their craftsmen were now gone, and the younger generation relied on automation and machines to accomplish less artistic goals. By the mid-1950s, most of these once-great manufacturers were closed.

Other marques survived. The European Alfa Romeo, Jaguar, Rolls-Royce, and Bentley somehow lasted, each taking a slightly different postwar path. The American Lincoln and Cadillac became less awe-inspiring but were produced in greater numbers. Packard's fate was less fortunate, however, as it merged with Studebaker before joining the departed Pierce-Arrow, Auburn, Cord, and Duesenberg.

By 1948 the classic era of automotive design was over. The social factors that created it and allowed it to flourish—fabulous wealth and a patronage of the arts—have long since disappeared. Computers and electronic driving aids in amorphous, indistinguishable vehicles have replaced the technological explosion that spurred these stunning motorcars. Flights of fancy and dreams of the future have fallen to economic pressures and environmental concerns. Left are these beautiful machines: sculptures of metal, glass, wood, and leather, preserved in museums and by devoted collectors—a testament to humankind's desire to create and excel.

Michael Furman
Photographer and author

THE UNITED STATES
OF AMERICA

1927 Kissel 8-75 Speedster

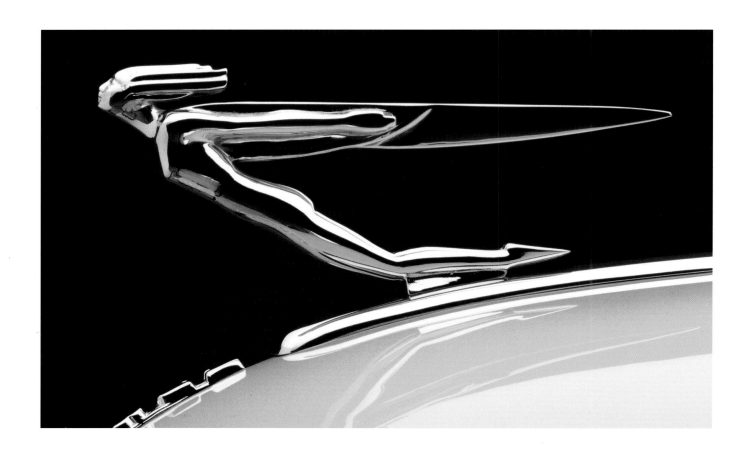

Hood Ornament
1935 Auburn 851 Speedster

Hood Ornament
1947 Cadillac Series 62 Convertible Coupé

1928 Cadillac 341A Dual Cowl Sport Phaeton

1931 Cord L-29

1931 Du Pont Model H

1930 Packard 745 Convertible Coupé
by Derham

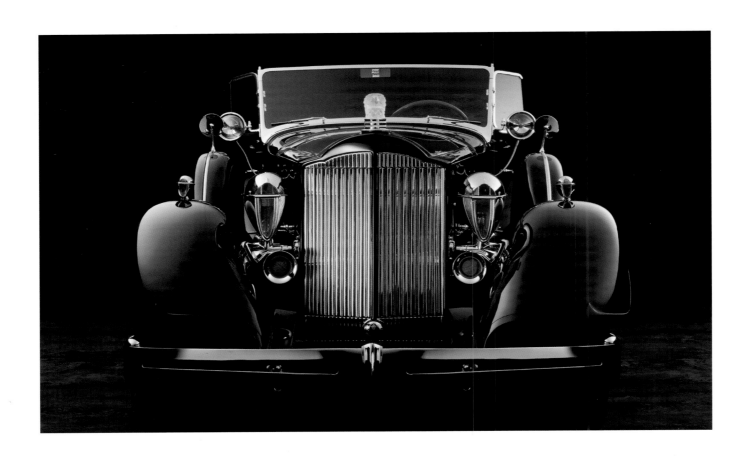

1934 Packard 1104 Dual Cowl Phaeton

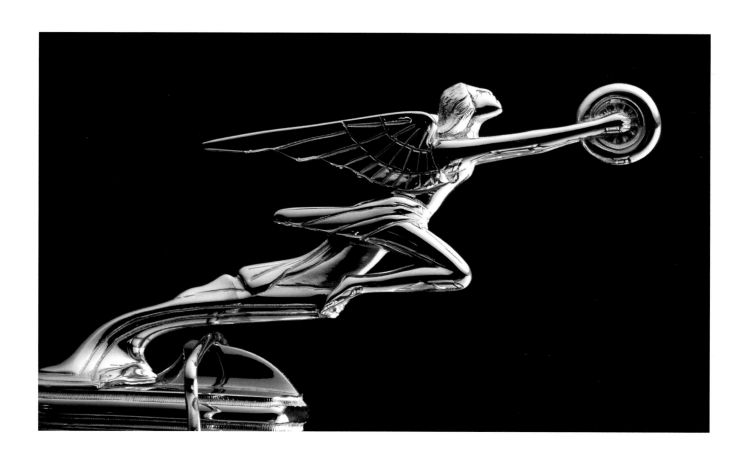

Hood Ornament
1930 Packard 745 Convertible Coupé
by Derham

1934 Packard 1108 Sport Phaeton
by LeBaron

1942 Packard Super-8 180 Darrin Convertible Victoria

Front Fender Detail
1934 Auburn Model 12-160 Salon

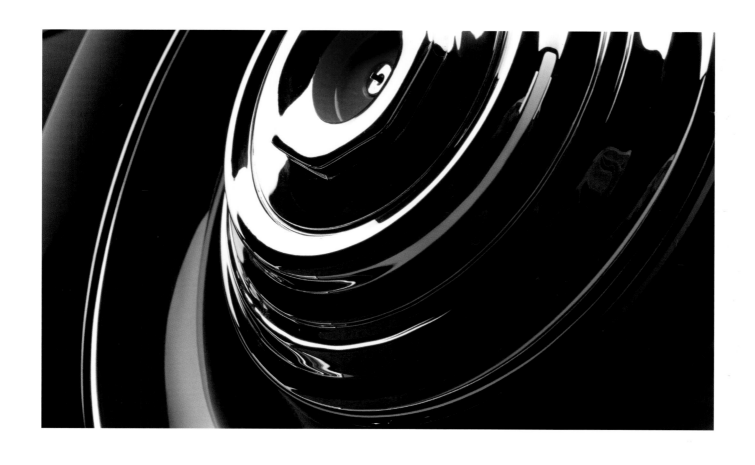

Fender Mounted Wheel Detail
1935 Duesenberg Model J Walker LeGrand Convertible Coupé

Body Detail
1926 Packard Model 326 Roadster

Fender Mounted Wheel Detail

1934 Packard 1104 Convertible Victoria

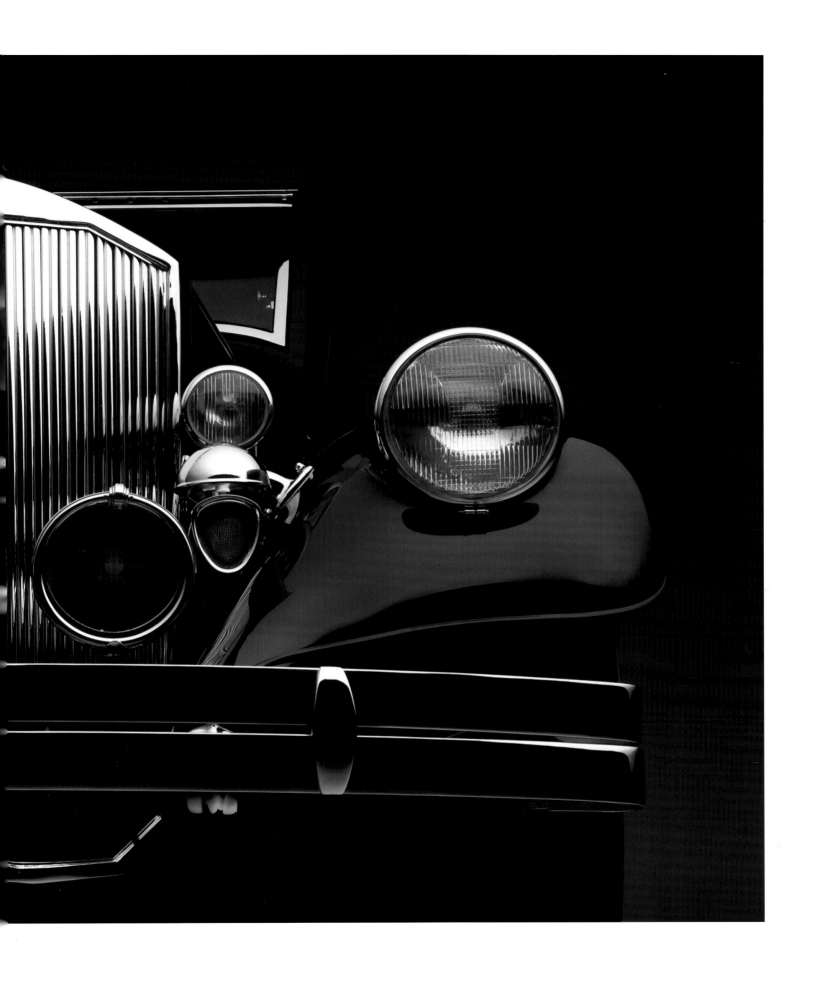

1933 Pierce-Arrow 1242 Convertible Coupé

1933 Pierce-Arrow 1242 Convertible Coupé

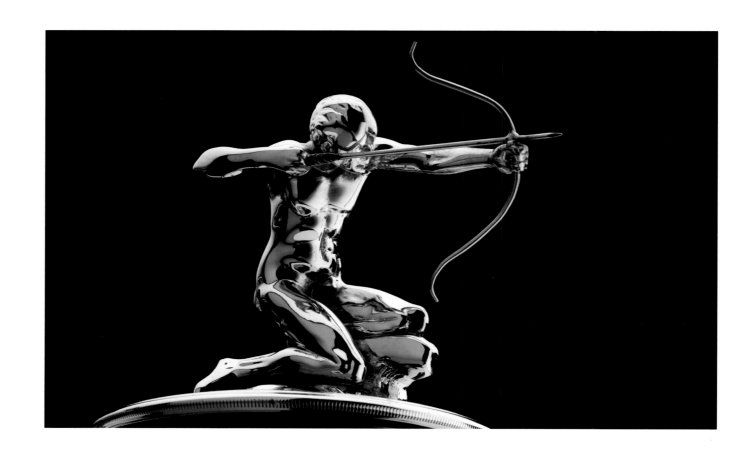

Hood Ornament

1933 Pierce-Arrow 1242 Convertible Coupé

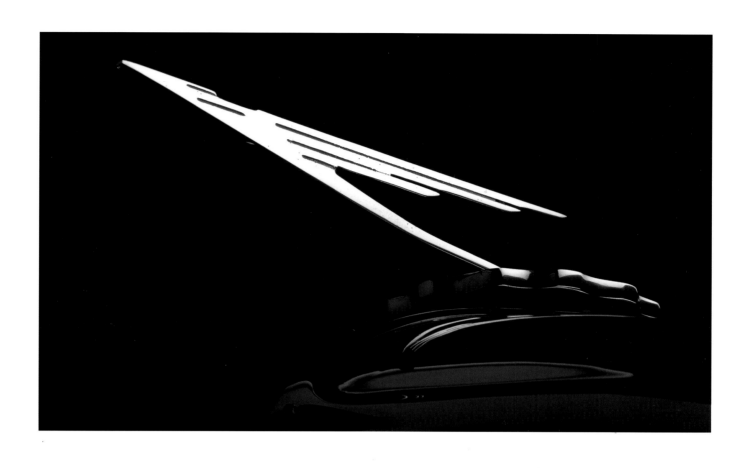

Hood Ornament
1931 Duesenberg Model SJ "French Speedster"
by Figoni et Falaschi

Radiator Shell and Grille Detail

1931 Duesenberg Model SJ "French Speedster"

by Figoni et Falaschi

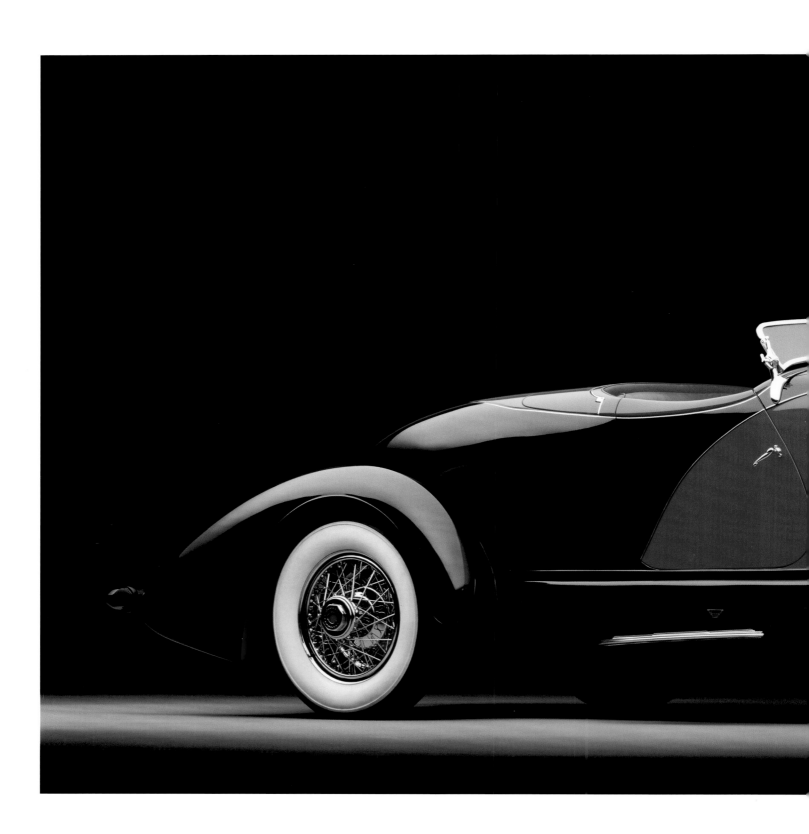

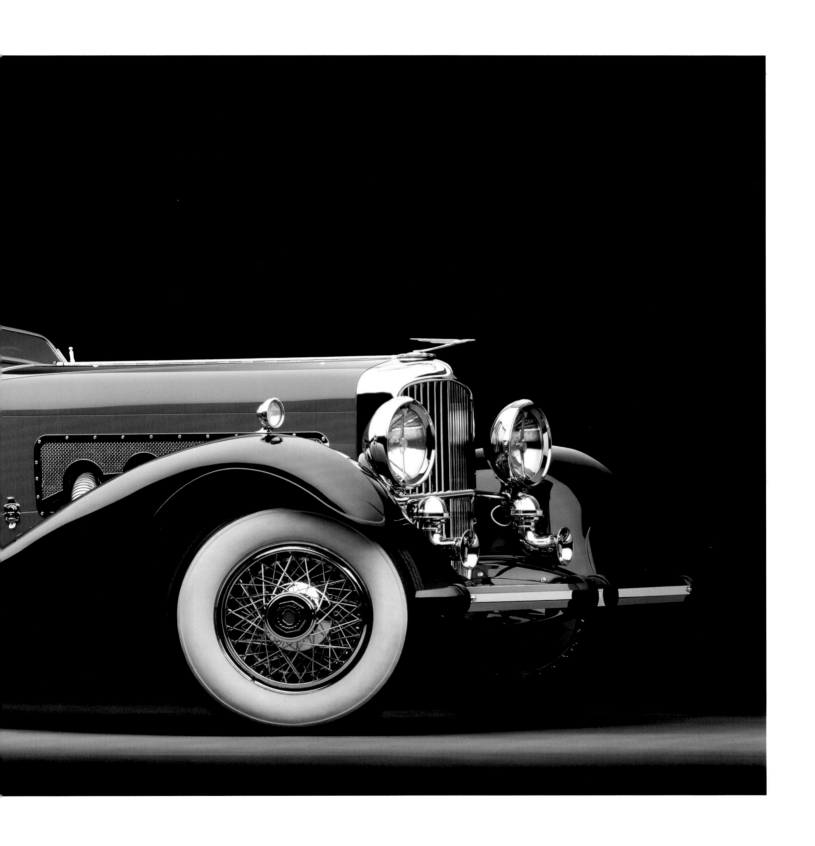

1931 Duesenberg Model SJ "French Speedster"
by Figoni et Falaschi

1935 Duesenberg Model SJ
by Bohman & Schwartz

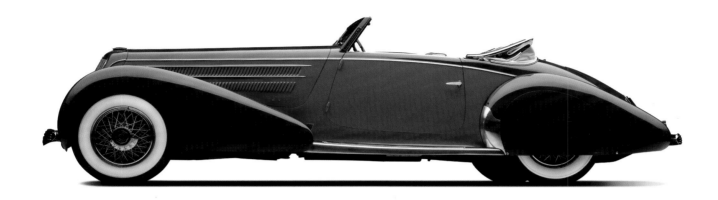

1935 Duesenberg Model SJ Convertible Victoria
by Graber

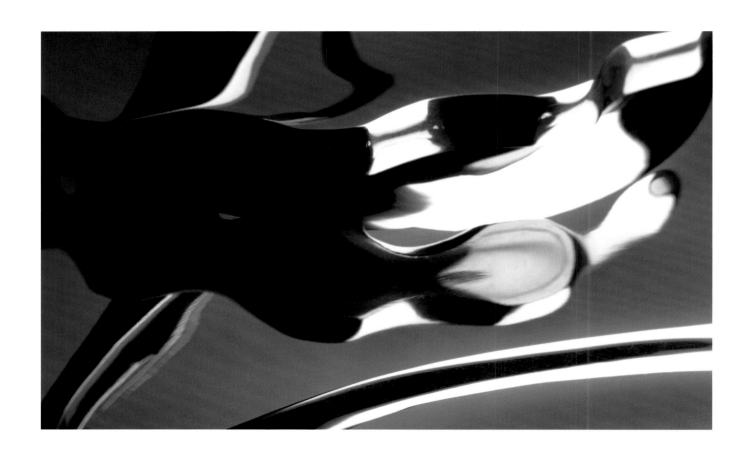

Radiator Detail
1931 Duesenberg Model SJ "French Speedster"
by Figoni et Falaschi

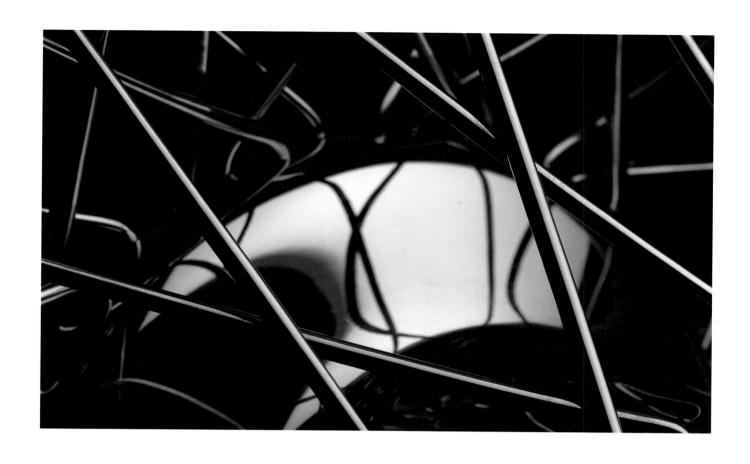

Wheel Detail
1931 Duesenberg Model SJ "French Speedster"
by Figoni et Falaschi

1935 Duesenberg Model J Walker LeGrand Convertible Coupé

Hood Ornament
1932 Stutz DV-32 Convertible

1929 Stutz Convertible Victoria
by Hibbard & Darrin

1928 Stutz BB Black Hawk Speedster

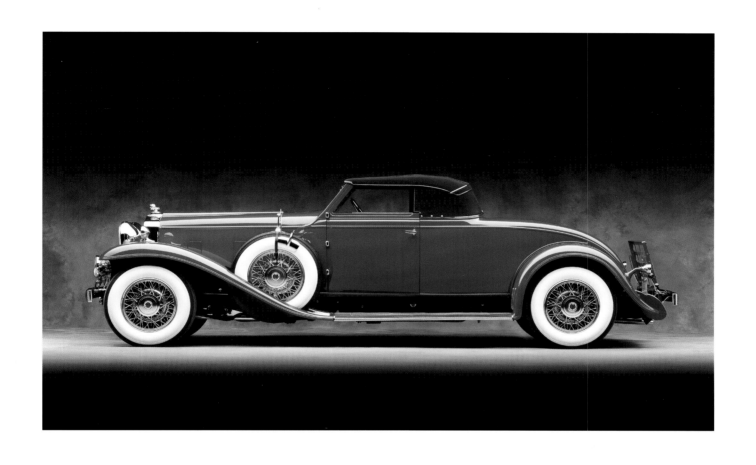

1932 Stutz DV-32 Convertible

1932 Chrysler Imperial Speedster
by LeBaron

1930 Ruxton

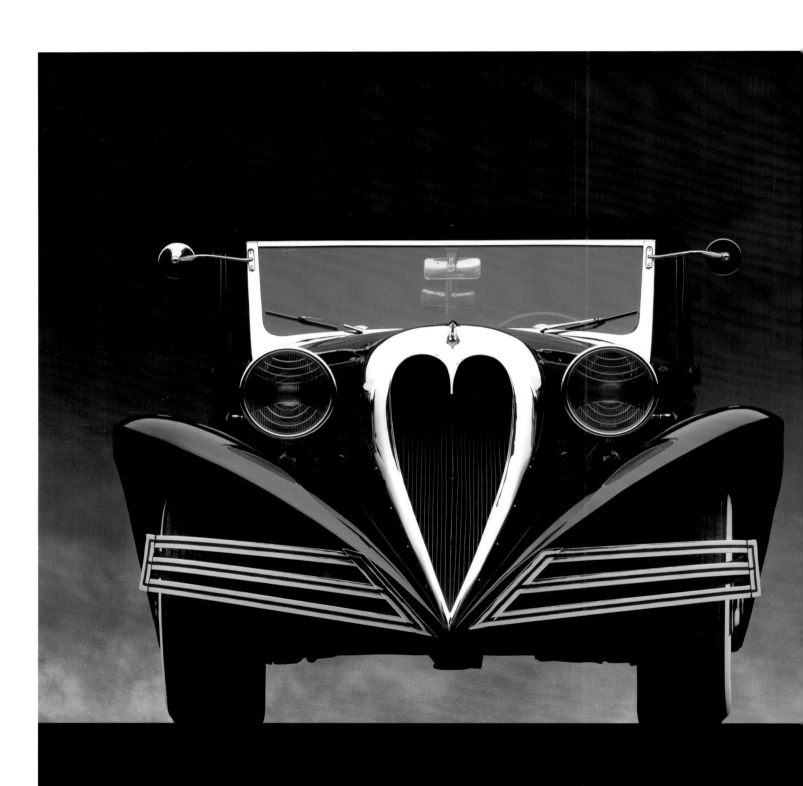

1935 Brewster Town Car (Ford V-8)

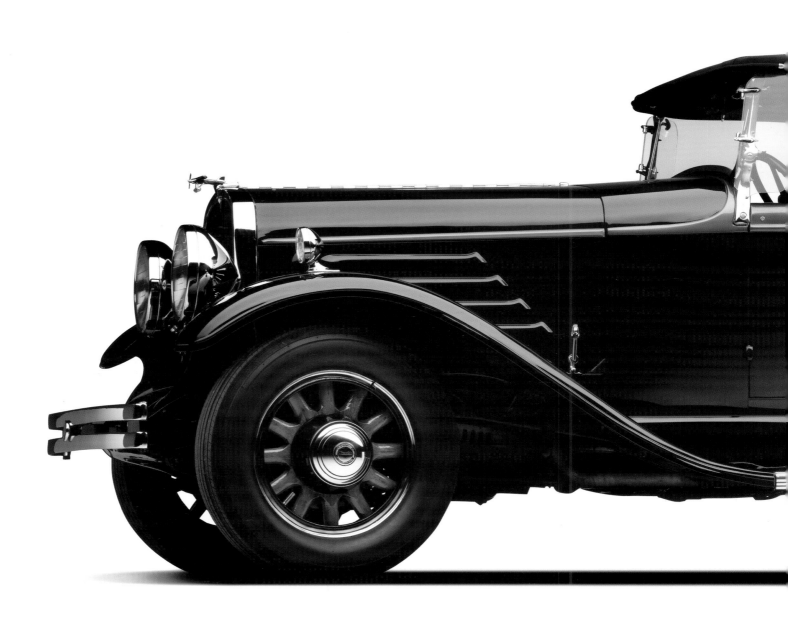

1930 Franklin Series 147 Sport Runabout

Radiator Badge and Grille Detail
1934 Studebaker Commander Coupé

Wheel Detail
1934 Studebaker Commander Coupé

1931 Studebaker President

Hood Ornament
1931 Studebaker President

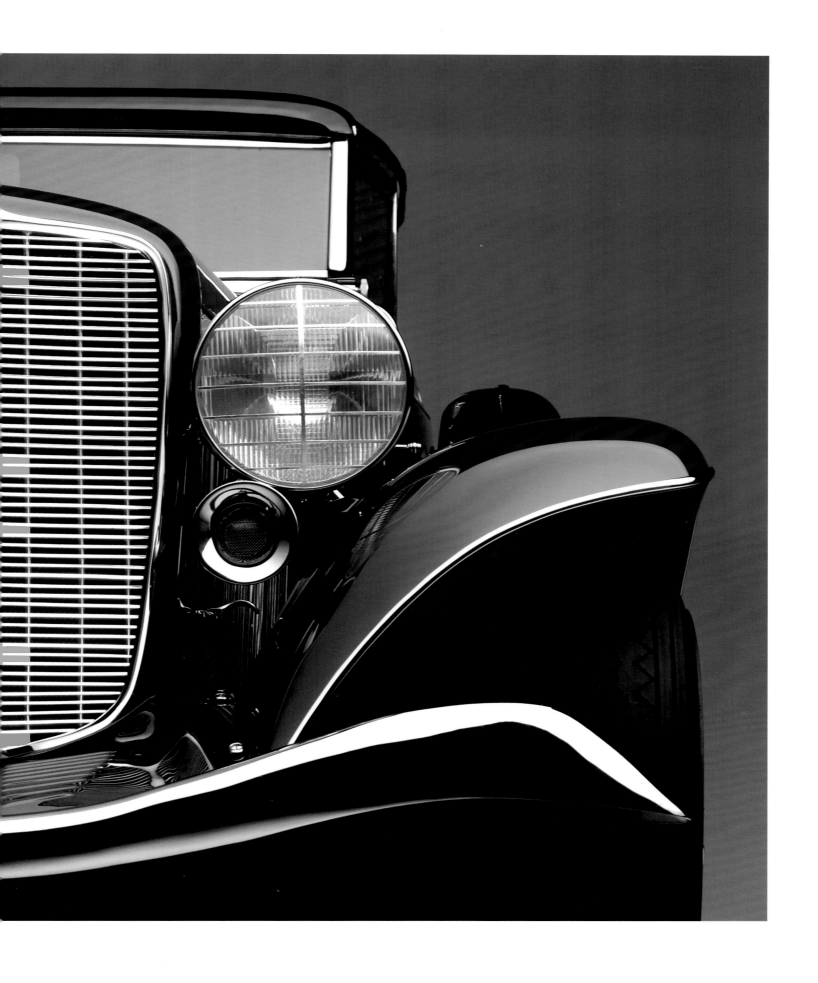

1934 Auburn Model 12-160 Salon

1937 Cord 812 Sportsman

Louver Reflection Detail
1936 Cord 810

Rear Fender Detail
1936 Cord 810

1928 Auburn 8-115 Speedster

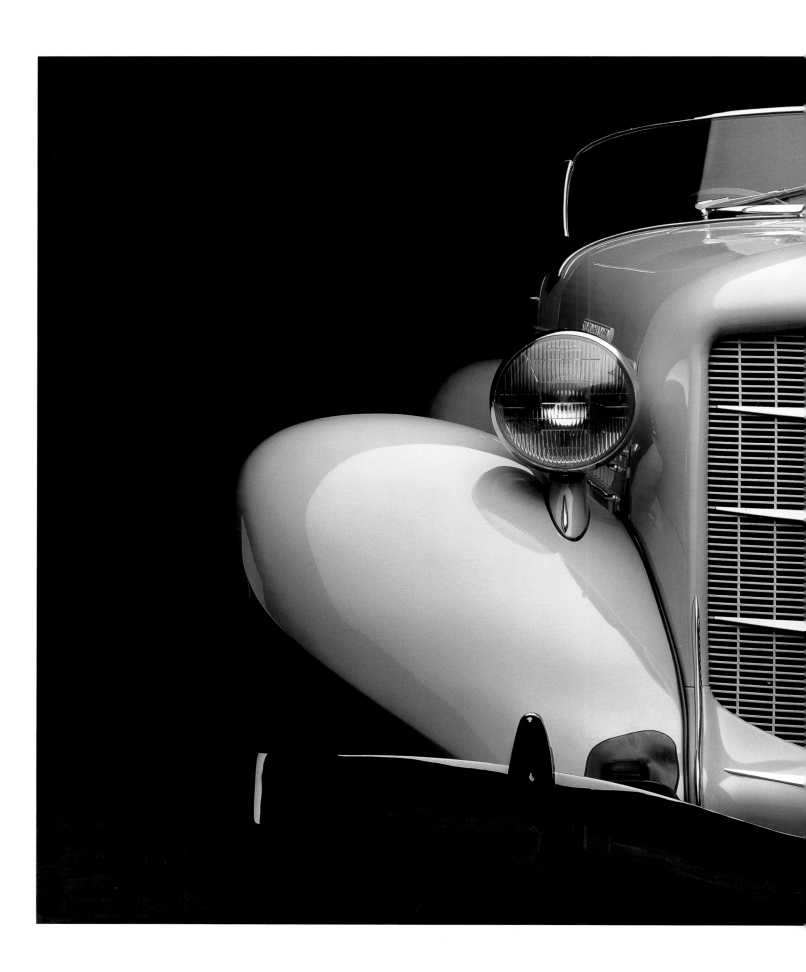

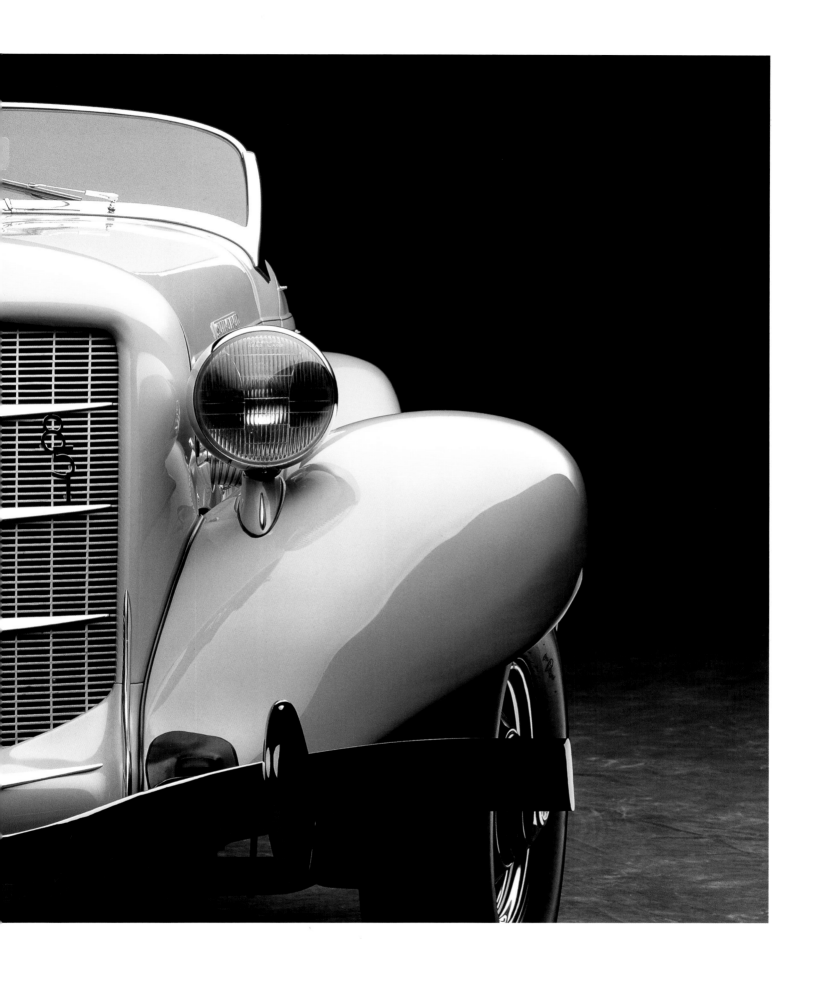

1935 Auburn 851 Speedster

1935 Auburn 851 Speedster

Headlight Detail
1935 Auburn 851 Speedster

Supercharger Pipes Detail
1935 Auburn 851 Speedster

1936 Stout Scarab

1940 LaSalle Series 52 Convertible

1930 LaSalle 7-Passenger Touring Car
by Fleetwood

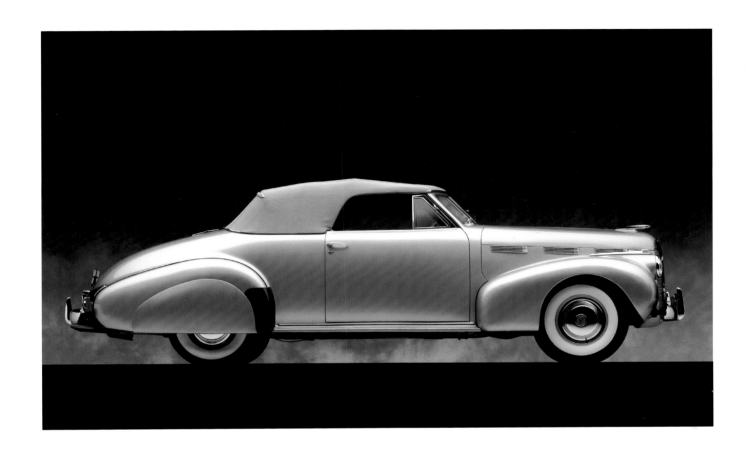

1940 LaSalle Series 52 Convertible

Hood Ornament
1937 Cadillac V16 Fleetwood

1936 Cadillac V16 Fleetwood Special Roadster

Front Wheel Detail
1936 Cadillac V16 Fleetwood Special Roadster

Steering Wheel Detail
1936 Cadillac V16 Fleetwood Special Roadster

Hood Ornament
1928 Cadillac 341A Dual Cowl Sport Phaeton

Hood Badge
1947 Cadillac Series 62 Convertible Coupé

Tire Tread
1932 Stutz DV-32 Convertible

Badge and Grille Detail
1937 Cadillac V16 Fleetwood

1937 Cadillac V16 Fleetwood

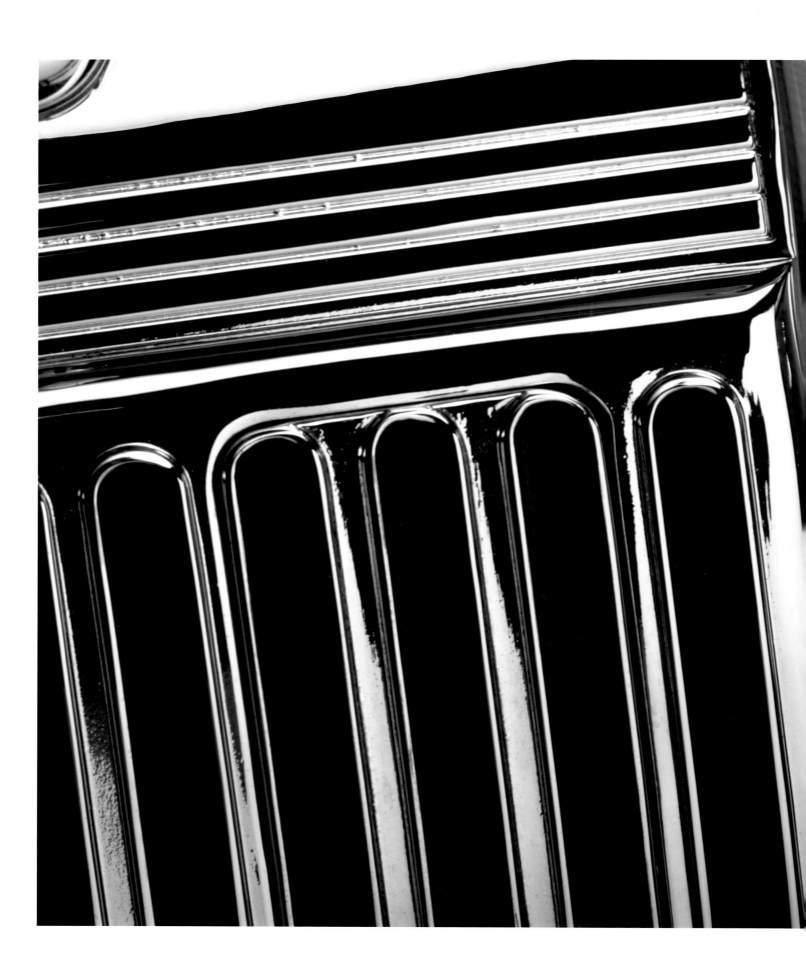

Dashboard Detail
1947 Cadillac Series 62 Convertible Coupé

1947 Cadillac Series 62 Convertible Coupé

1948 Chrysler Town and Country

1932 Chrysler Imperial Speedster CH

Steering Wheel Detail
1932 Chrysler Imperial Speedster CH

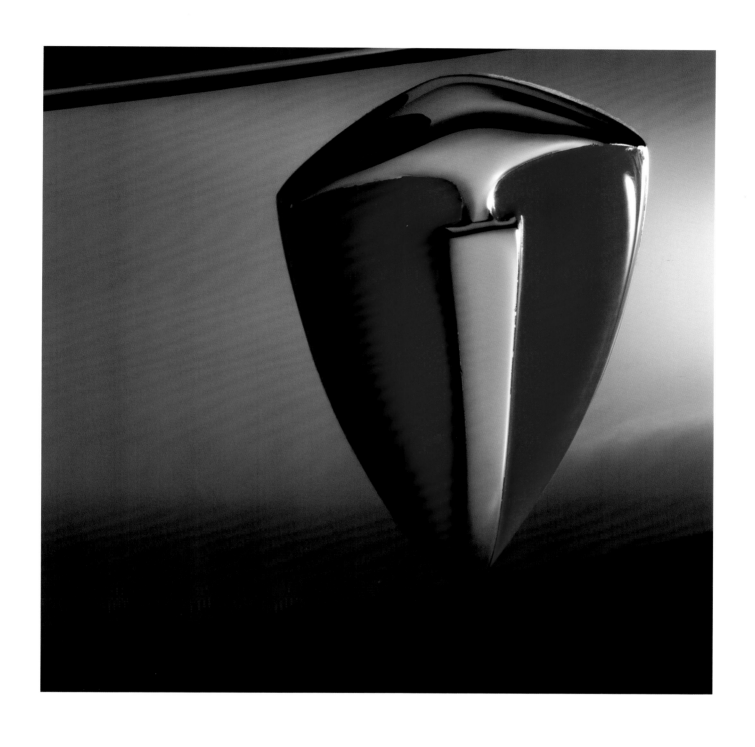

Bumper Detail

1932 Chrysler Imperial Speedster CH

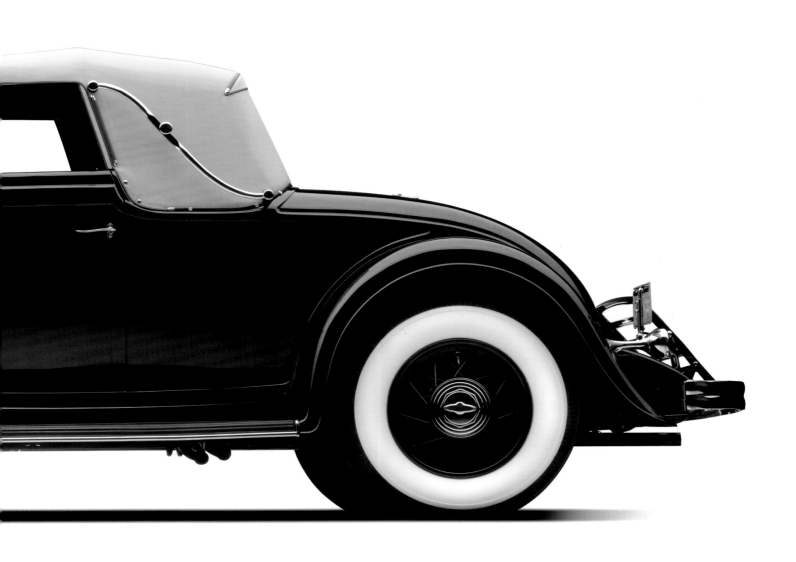

1932 Lincoln KB Model 248 Convertible Roadster
by LeBaron

Hood Ornament
1932 Lincoln KB Model 248 Convertible Roadster
by LeBaron

Fender Mounted Wheel Detail
1932 Lincoln KB Model 248 Convertible Roadster
by LeBaron

1940 Lincoln Continental Convertible

GREAT BRITAIN

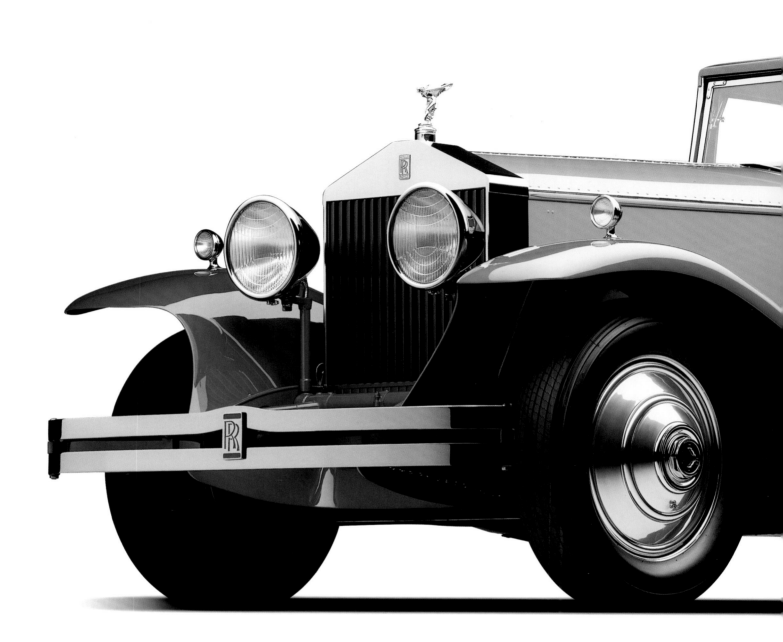

1931 Rolls-Royce Phantom I Regent
by Brewster

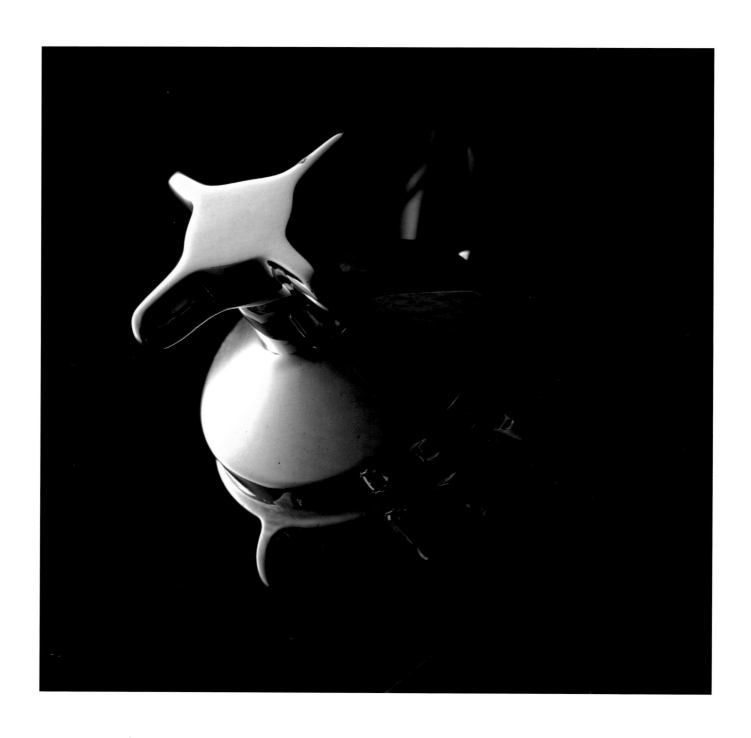

Gas Cap
1927 Rolls-Royce Phantom I Brougham
by Charles Clark & Sons of Wolverhampton

Rear Door Detail

1927 Rolls-Royce Phantom I Brougham

by Charles Clark & Sons of Wolverhampton

1931 Rolls-Royce Phantom II Newmarket
by Brewster

1931 Rolls-Royce Phantom II Continental Close Coupled 4-Some
by Mulliner

1934 Rolls-Royce 20/25 Shooting Brake
by Joseph Cockshoot

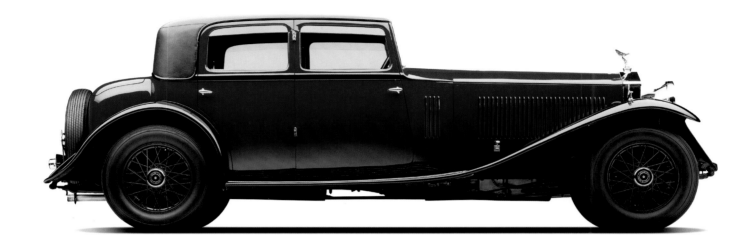

1932 Rolls-Royce Phantom II Continental Sports Saloon
by Mulliner

1936 Rolls-Royce Phantom III Coupé
by Barker

Fender Mounted Wheel Detail

1931 Rolls-Royce Phantom I Regent

by Brewster

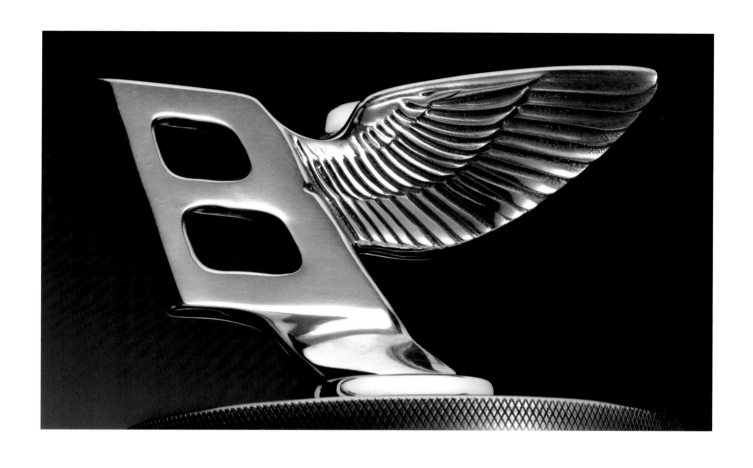

Hood Ornament
1937 Bentley 4 1/4-Litre Gurney Nutting Sedanca Coupé

1929 Bentley 4 1/2-Litre Harrison Tourer

MILES-P

8 9

120

BRITISH
MADE

JAE

Speedometer Detail
1929 Bentley 4 1/2-Litre Harrison Tourer

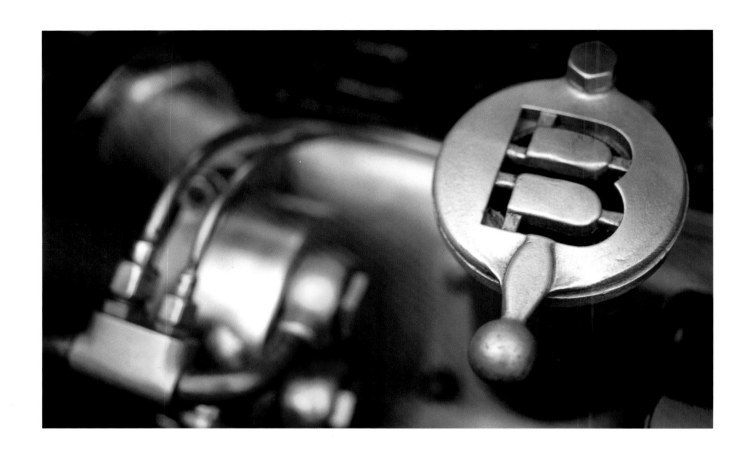

Engine Detail
1927 Bentley 3-Litre

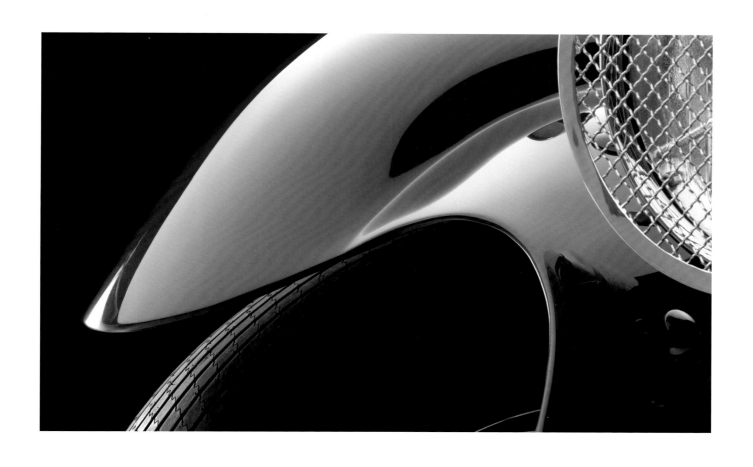

Fender Detail
1929 Bentley 4 1/2-Litre Harrison Tourer

Seat Detail
1931 Rolls-Royce Phantom II Newmarket
by Brewster

Wheel Detail

1931 Rolls-Royce Phantom II Newmarket

by Brewster

1937 Bentley 4 1/4-Litre Gurney Nutting Sedanca Coupé

1934 Bentley 3 1/2-Litre Fixed Head Saloon
by Freestone & Webb

1948 Jaguar 3 1/2-Litre Saloon

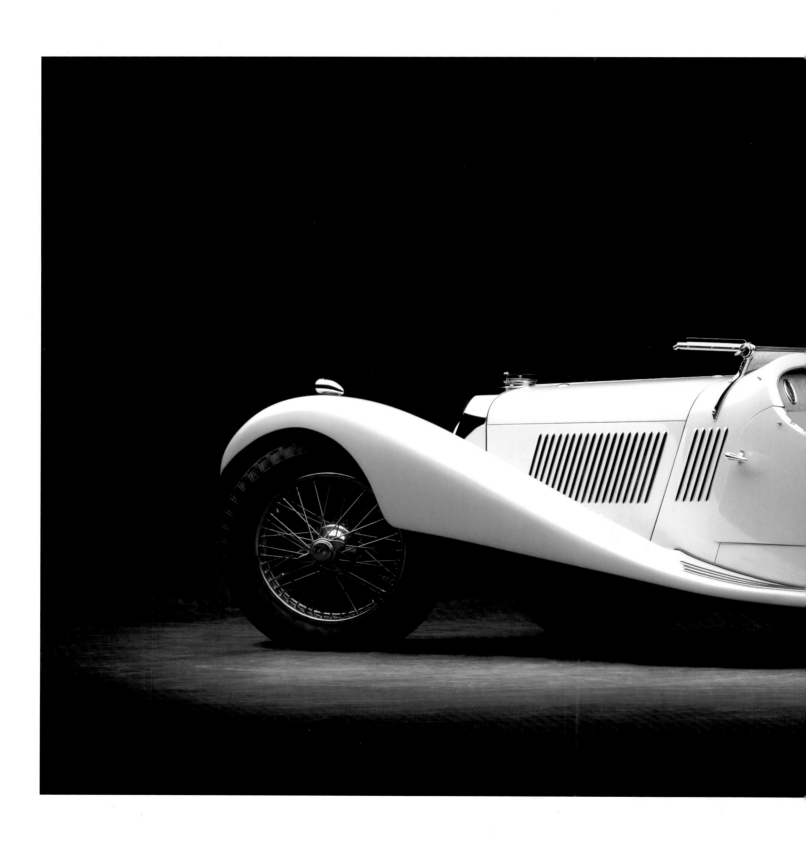

1933 Squire

by Van Den Plas

Hood Ornament
1931 Rolls-Royce Phantom I Regent
by Brewster

Bumper Detail
1931 Rolls-Royce Phantom II Newmarket
by Brewster

THE CONTINENT

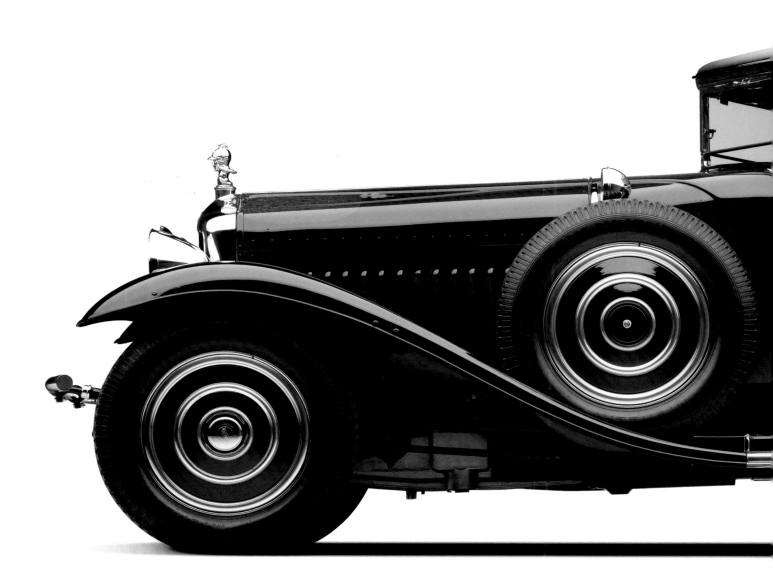

1927 Minerva AK
by LeBaron

Wheel Detail
1927 Minerva AK
by LeBaron

Door Detail
1927 Minerva AK
by LeBaron

Hood Ornament
1927 Minerva AK
by LeBaron

Hood Badge
1930 Isotta-Fraschini Model 8-A
by Castagna

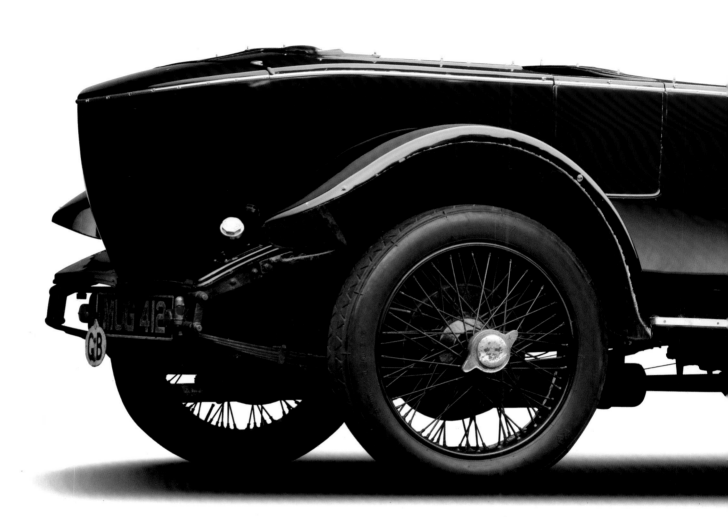

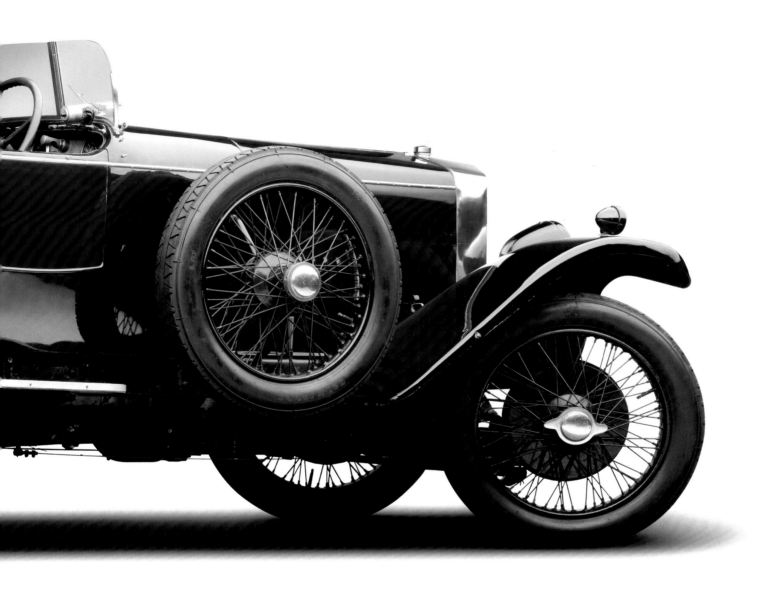

1925 Alfa Romeo RLSS

1938 Alfa Romeo 8C-2900B
by Touring

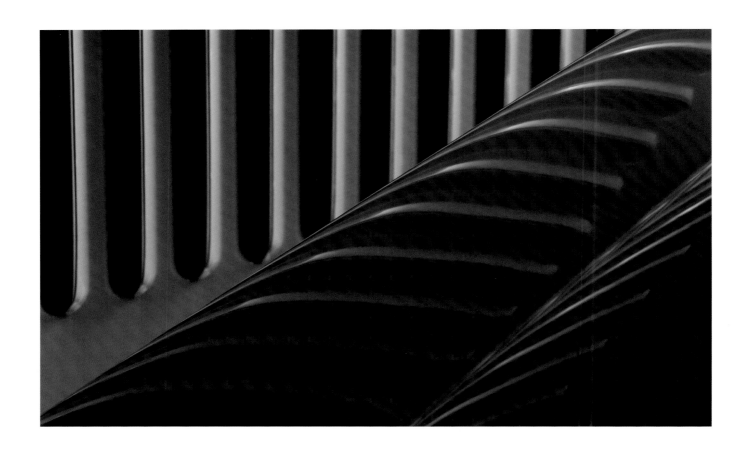

Body Detail
1930 Isotta-Fraschini Model 8-A
by Castagna

Radiator Detail
1925 Alfa Romeo RLSS

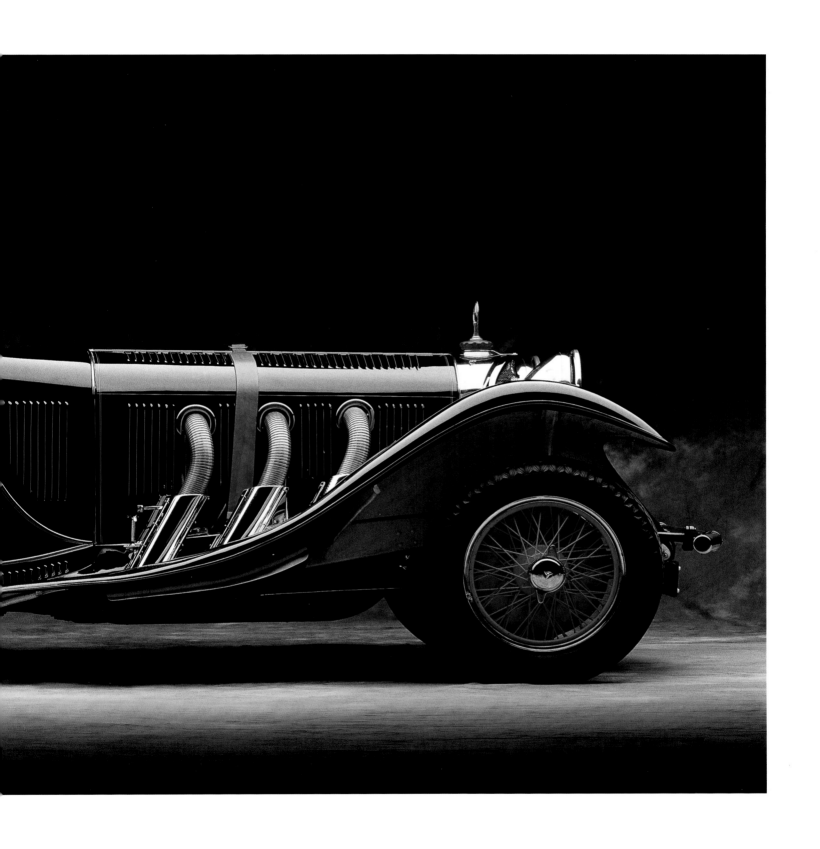

1928 Mercedes-Benz S

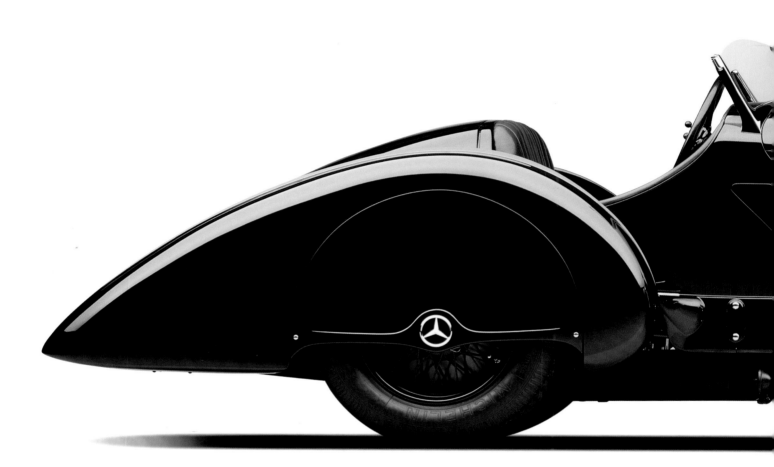

1930 Mercedes-Benz SSK "Count Trossi"

Wheel Detail
1930 Mercedes-Benz SSK "Count Trossi"

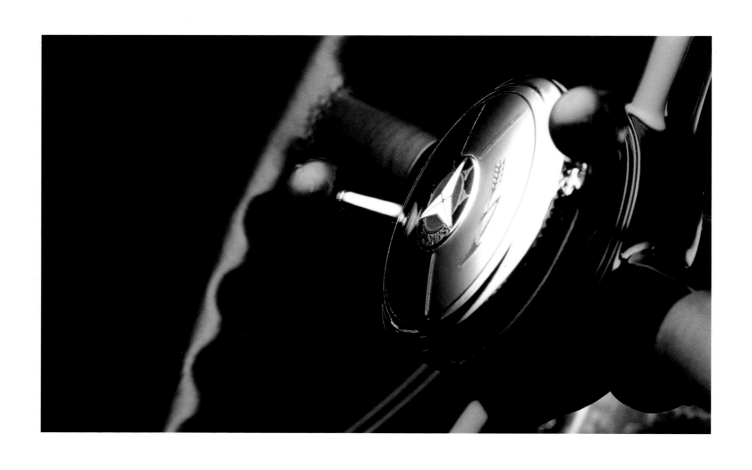

Steering Wheel Detail
1930 Mercedes-Benz SSK "Count Trossi"

Tachometer Detail
1930 Mercedes-Benz SSK "Count Trossi"

Hood Ornament
1929 Mercedes-Benz SSK

Rear Deck Detail
1937 Mercedes-Benz 540 K Special Roadster

Running Board Detail
1937 Mercedes-Benz 540 K Special Roadster

Lights and Horns Detail
1937 Mercedes-Benz 540 K Special Roadster

1938 Mercedes-Benz 540 K Cabriolet A

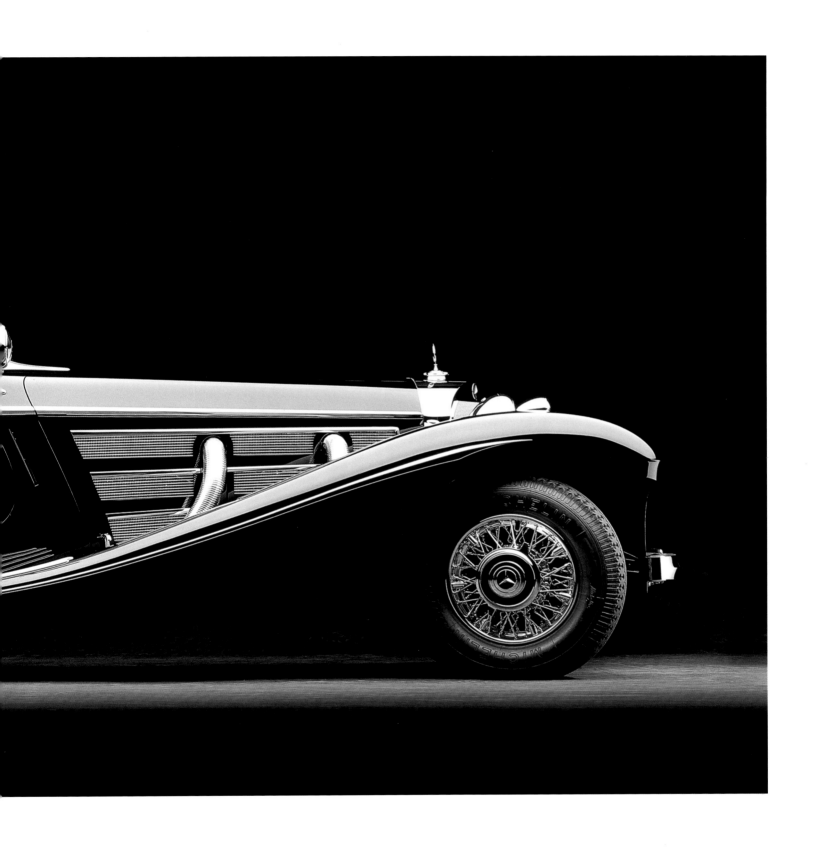

1937 Mercedes-Benz 540 K Special Roadster

Engine Detail
1937 Mercedes-Benz 540 K Special Roadster

Windscreen Detail
1930 Mercedes-Benz SSK "Count Trossi"

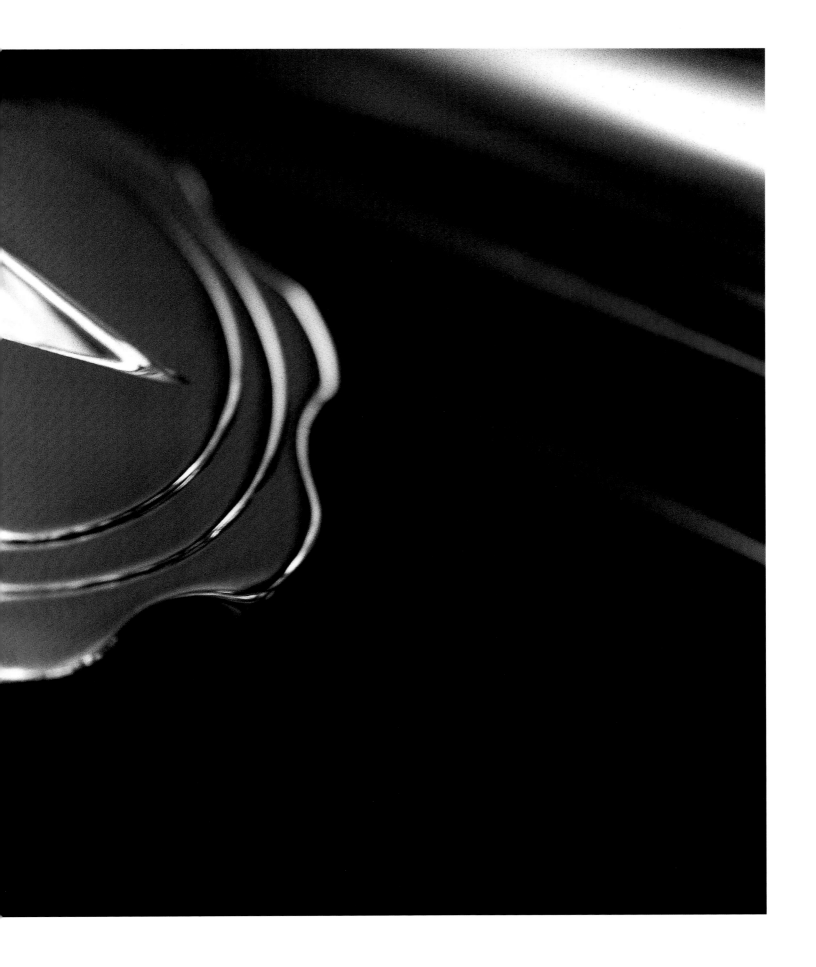

Engine Detail
1938 Mercedes-Benz 540 K Cabriolet A

Engine Detail
1939 Horch 853A Cabriolet

Rear Deck Detail
1937 BMW 327 Cabriolet

Rear Fender Detail
1938 BMW 328

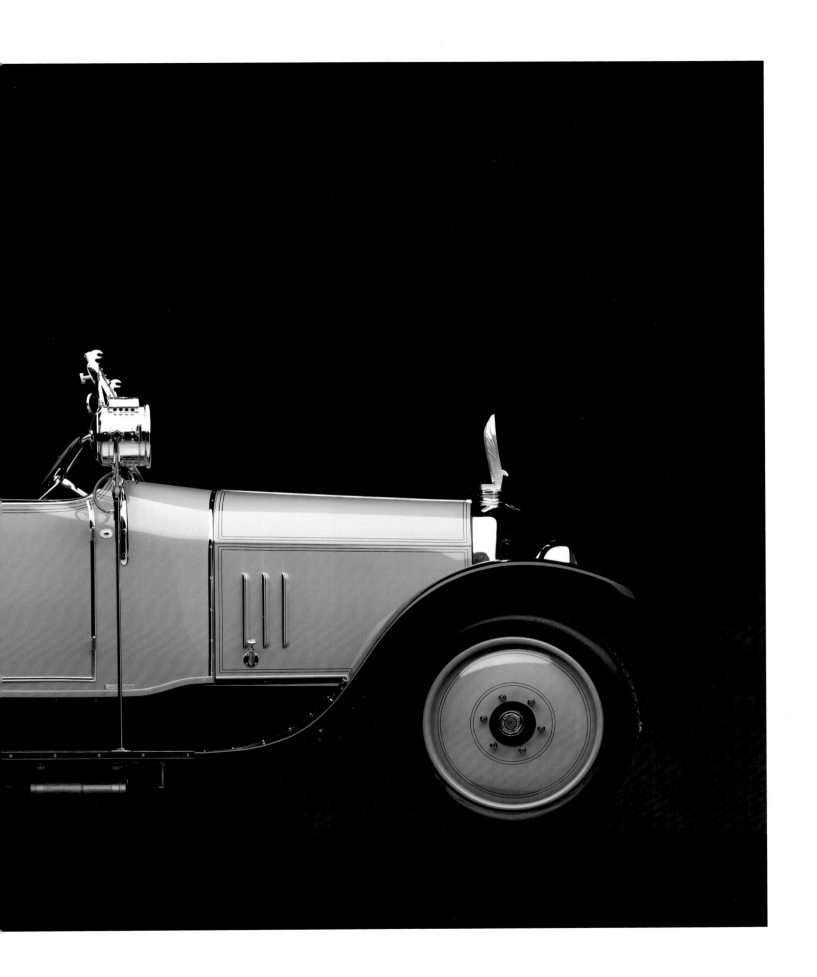

1925 Voisin C3L Berline Transformable

by J. Rothschild & Son

Radiator Badge
1937 Delahaye 135M
by Figoni et Falaschi

1937 Delahaye 135M
by Figoni et Falaschi

Door Detail

1932 Delage D8-SS

by Fernandez & Darrin

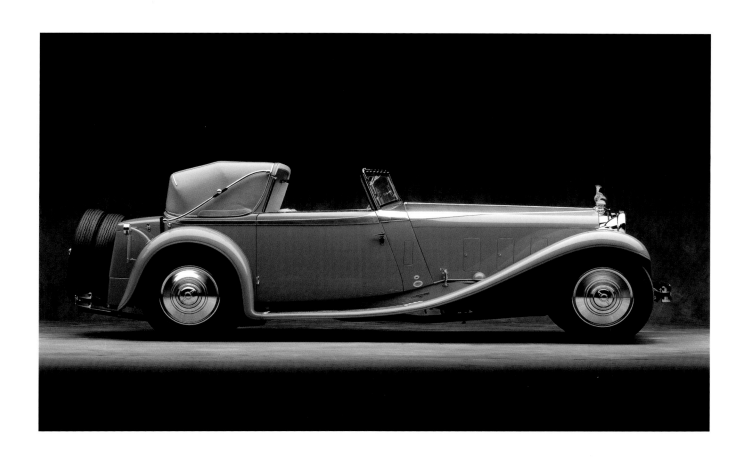

1932 Delage D8-SS

by Fernandez & Darrin

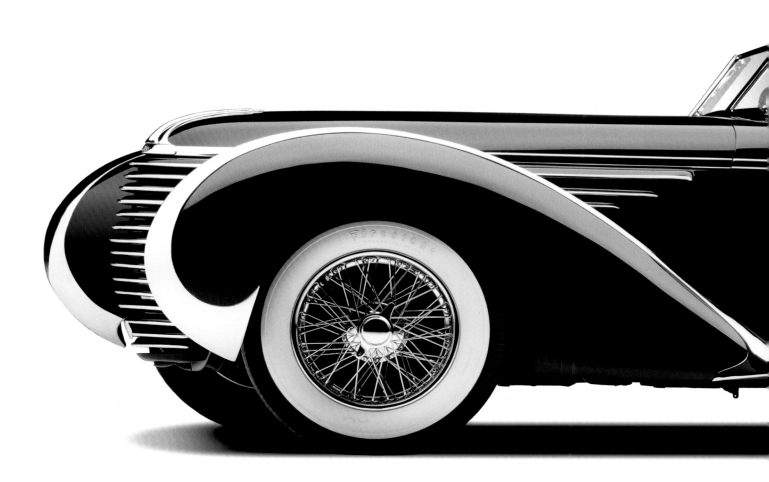

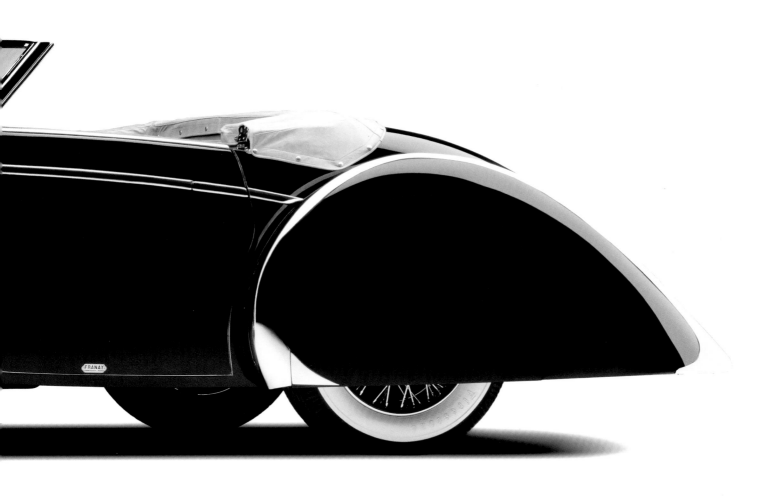

1947 Delahaye 135M Franay Cabriolet

1947 Delahaye 135MS
by Figoni et Falaschi

Door Detail
1947 Delahaye 135MS
by Figoni et Falaschi

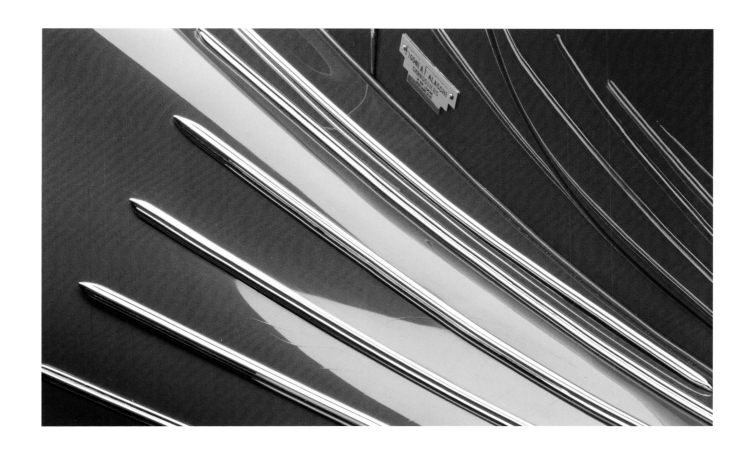

Running Board Detail
1947 Delahaye 135MS
by Figoni et Falaschi

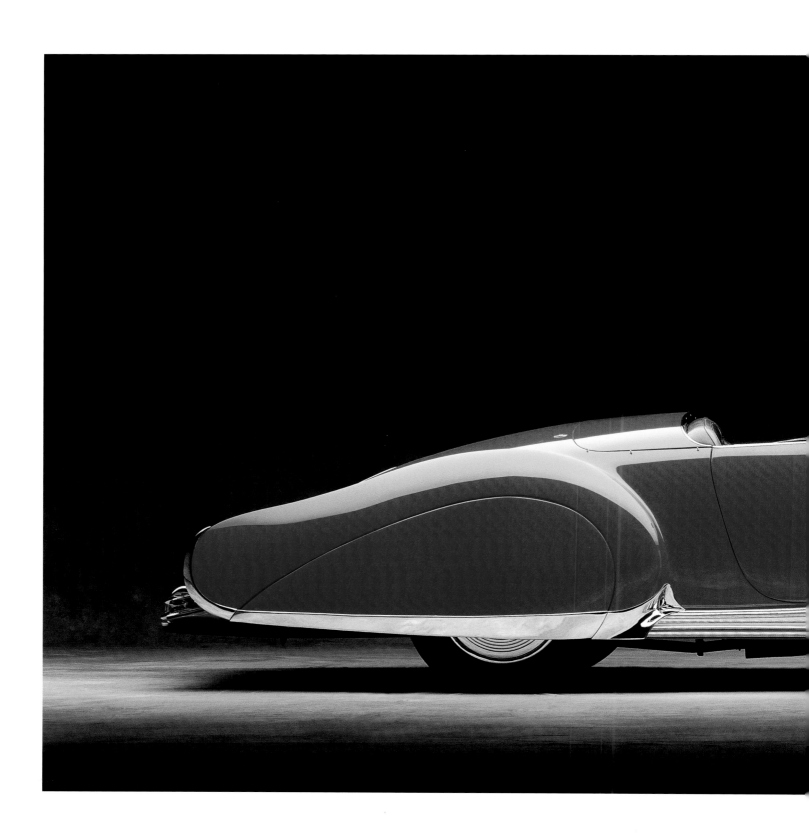

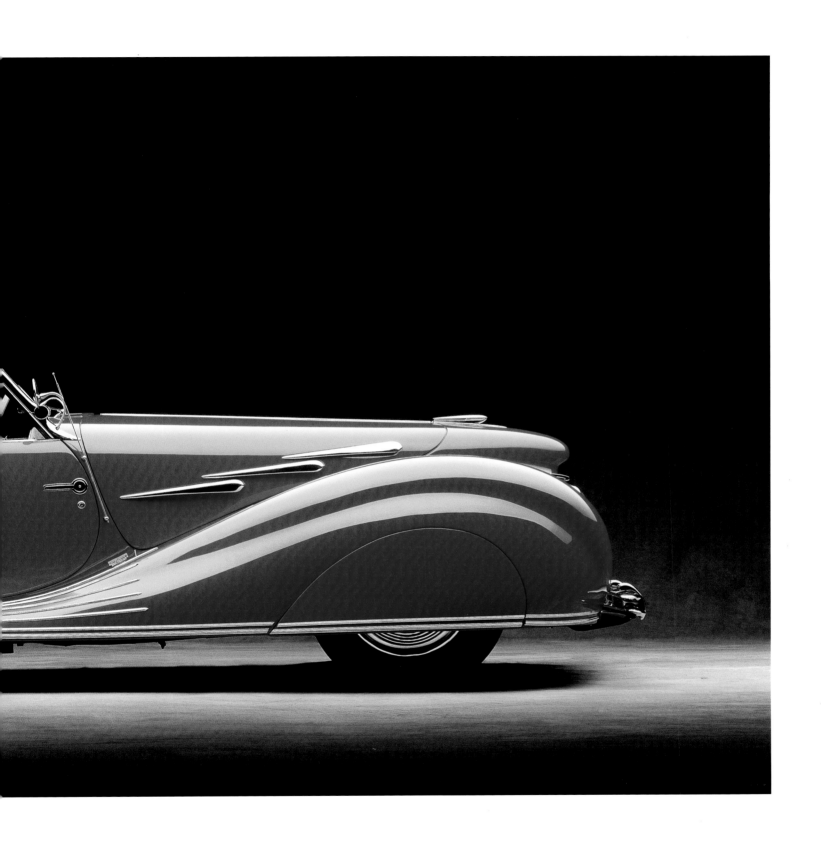

1947 Delahaye 135MS

by Figoni et Falaschi

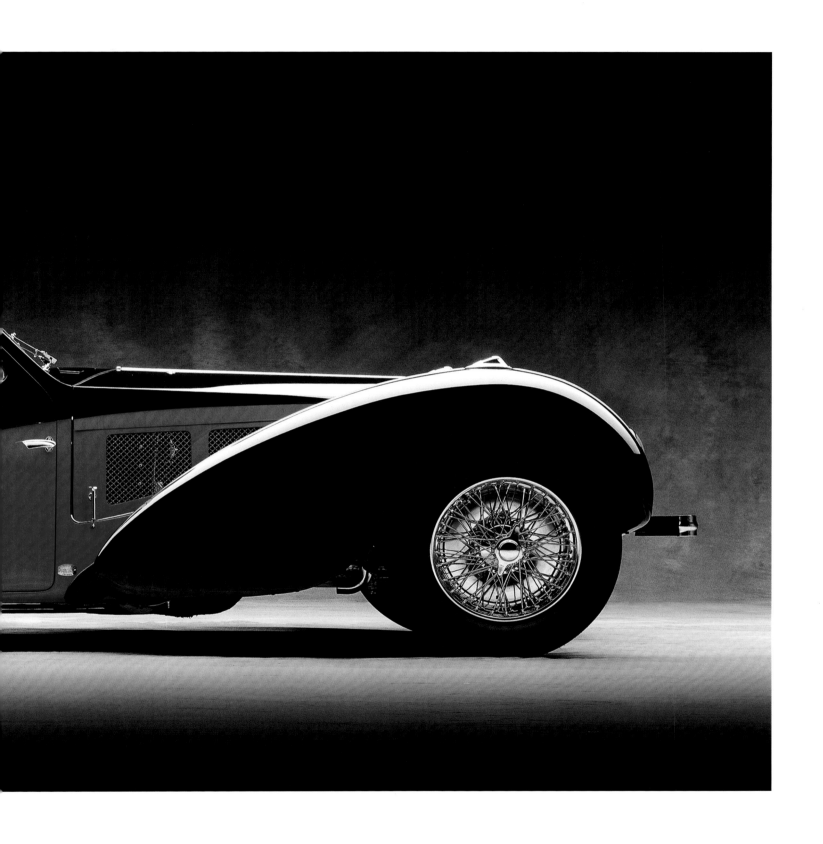

1937 Bugatti Type 57S Atalante

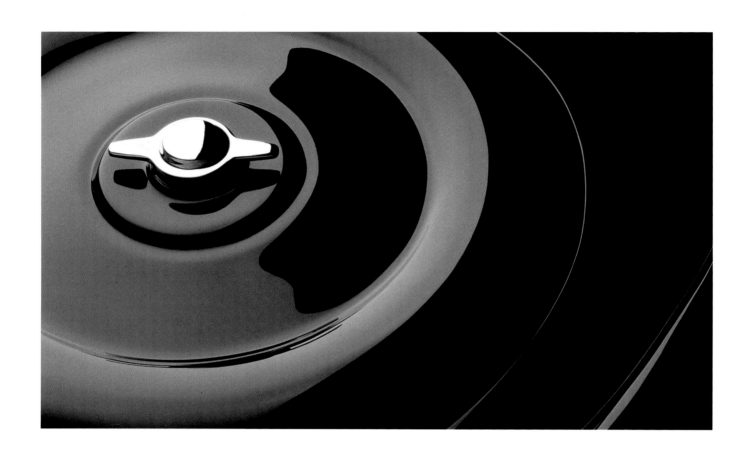

Rear Deck Detail
1937 Bugatti Type 57S Atalante

Rear Window Detail
1937 Bugatti Type 57S Atalante

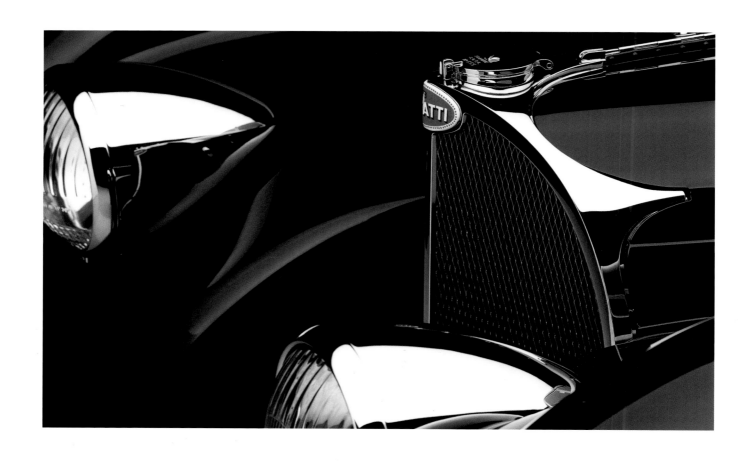

Front End Detail
1937 Bugatti Type 57S Atalante

Tailpipe Detail
1937 Bugatti Type 57S Atalante

1938 Delage D8-120 SS

by deVillars

Fender Detail
1938 Delage D8-120 SS
by deVillars

Radiator Badge
1938 Delage D8-120 SS
by deVillars

Tire Detail
1927 Bugatti Type 38A

Engine Detail
1927 Bugatti Type 38A

Lalique *Tête de Paon*

Lalique *Cinq Chevaux*

Bumper Detail
1934 Voisin C15 ets Saliot Roadster

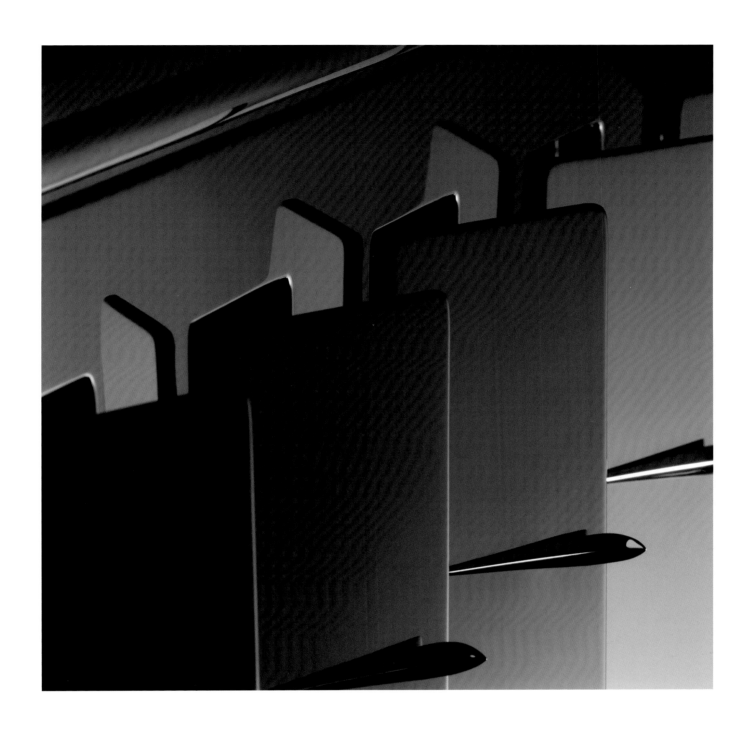

Hood Detail
1934 Voisin C15 ets Saliot Roadster

1934 Voisin C15 ets Saliot Roadster

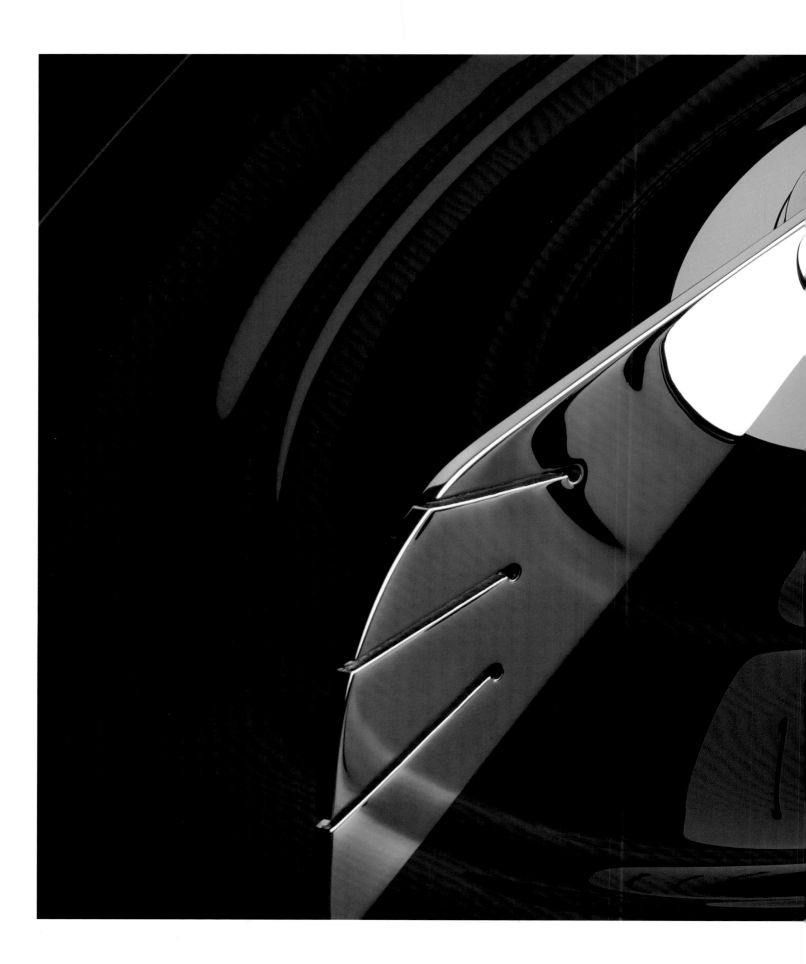

Rear Deck Detail
1934 Voisin C15 ets Saliot Roadster

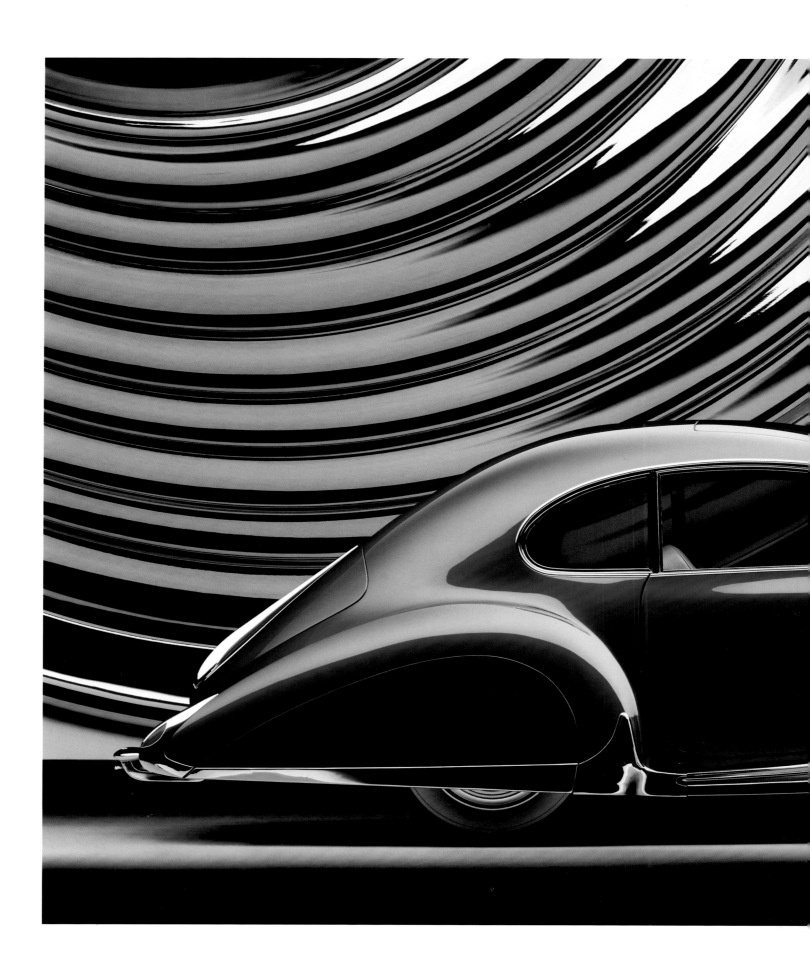

1938 Talbot-Lago T-23 "Teardrop Coupé"
by Figoni et Falaschi

1947 Delahaye 135MS Roadster

by Henri Chapron

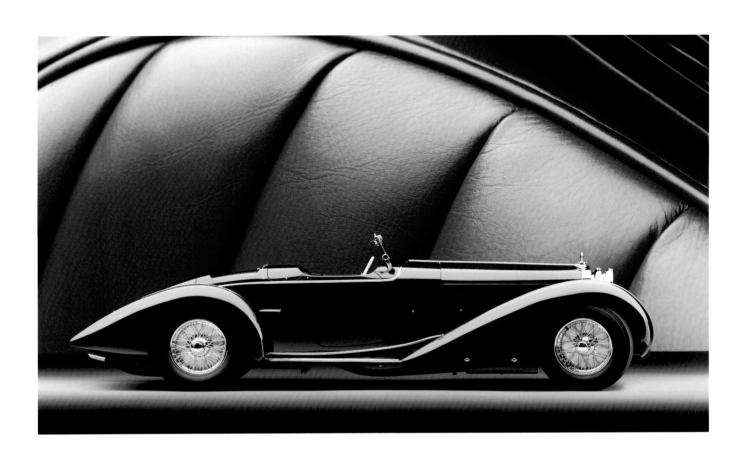

1932 Delage D8-SS Speedster

by Letourneur et Marchand

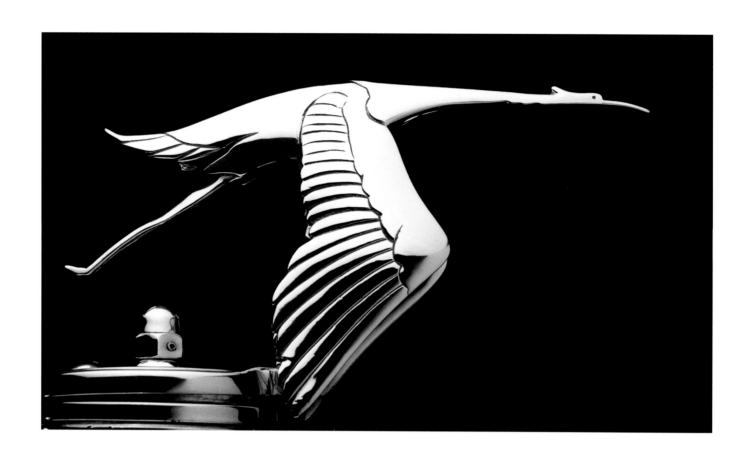

Hood Ornament
1928 Hispano-Suiza H-6C

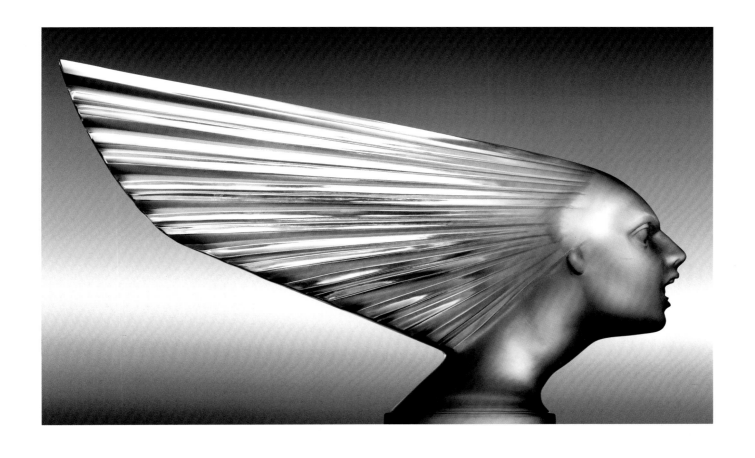

Lalique *Victoire*

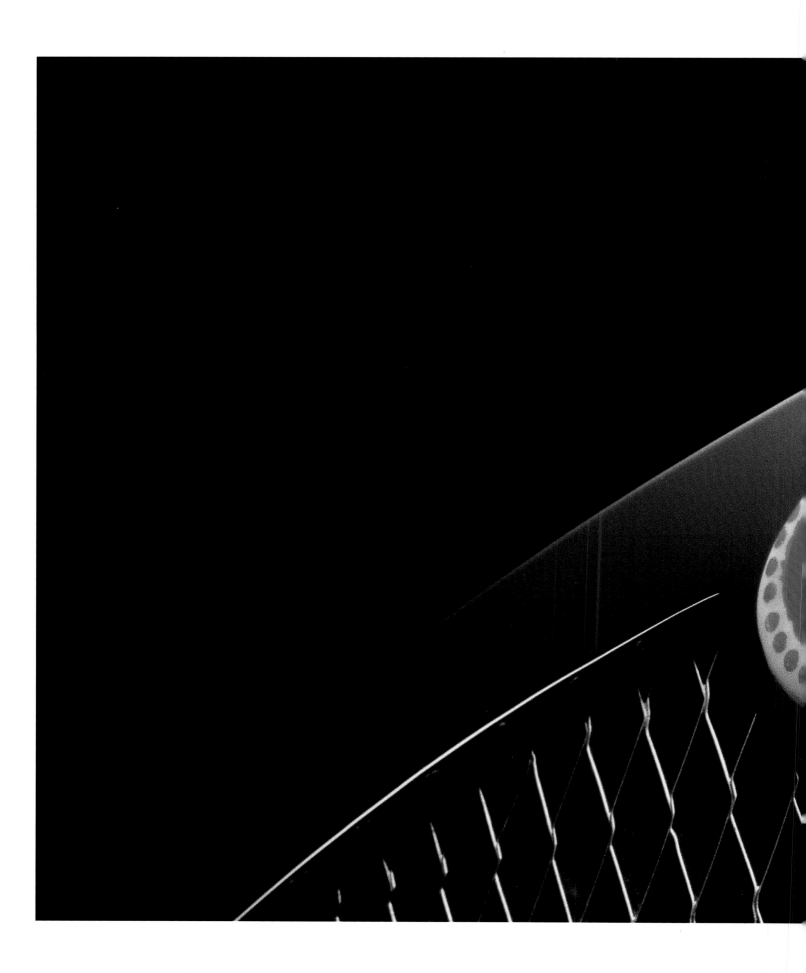

Radiator Badge
1938 Bugatti Type 57SC Atlantic Coupé

1938 Bugatti Type 57SC Atlantic Coupé

1938 Bugatti Type 57SC Atlantic Coupé

1938 Bugatti Type 57SC Atlantic Coupé

Interior Detail
1938 Bugatti Type 57SC Atlantic Coupé

Door Detail
1938 Bugatti Type 57SC Atlantic Coupé

Engine Scraping Detail
1938 Bugatti Type 57SC Atlantic Coupé

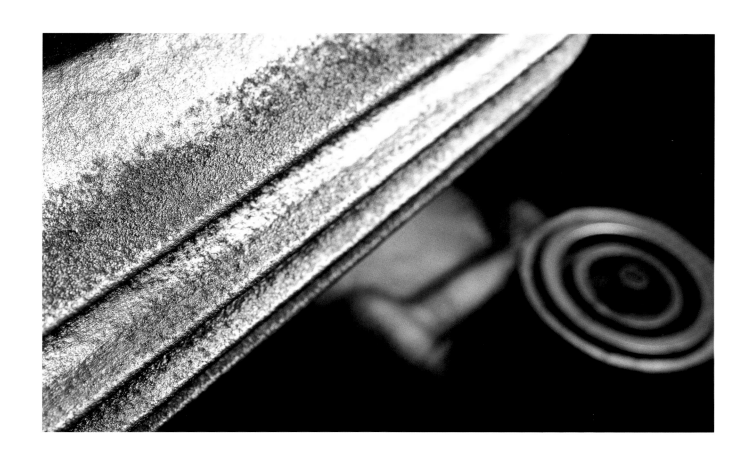

Engine Detail
1938 Bugatti Type 57SC Atlantic Coupé

Headlight and Fender Detail
1938 Bugatti Type 57SC Atlantic Coupé

1937 Dubonnet Hispano H-6C Xenia

by Saoutchik

Grille Detail
1937 Dubonnet Hispano H-6C Xenia
by Saoutchik

239

Steering Wheel Detail
1937 Dubonnet Hispano H-6C Xenia
by Saoutchik

Wheel Detail
1937 Dubonnet Hispano H-6C Xenia
by Saoutchik

Dashboard Detail

1937 Dubonnet Hispano H-6C Xenia

by Saoutchik

1937 Dubonnet Hispano H-6C Xenia

by Saoutchik

Body Detail
1937 Dubonnet Hispano H-6C Xenia
by Saoutchik

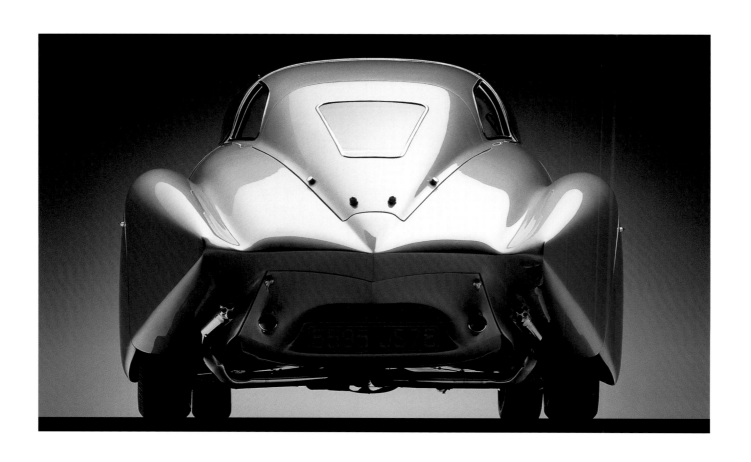

1937 Dubonnet Hispano H-6C Xenia

by Saoutchik

Since 1910 Alfa Romeo has produced some of the finest competition and road cars in the world. Originally founded as A.L.F.A. (Anonima Lombardo Fabbrica Automobili), the name was changed in 1915, when industrialist Nicola Romeo took control of the company. The marque quickly found success in Grand Prix racing, winning its first race on the Circuit of Mugello in 1920. From there, a succession of great machines from esteemed Alfa Romeo designers would dominate racing for twenty years.

1925 ALFA ROMEO RLSS

The RLSS was the culmination of the RL series designed by Guiseppe Meriosi. This chassis was adapted to a broad range of body styles, from two-seaters to limousines.

[pages 156–157, 161]

1938 ALFA ROMEO 8C-2900B
by Touring

Vittorio Jano was hired away from Fiat in 1923 to create Grand Prix cars for Nicola Romeo. Jano was immediately successful. His earliest design, the P2, won its first race at Lyons in August 1924. And the legacy continued with Jano's legendary 1750 and 8C-2300 designs, which garnered multiple victories at Le Mans and the Mille Miglia.

The 2900 was the 8C series' most powerful and one of the most beautiful designs to grace a race/touring car. It featured a straight-8-cylinder alloy engine with double overhead camshafts and twin superchargers—sophisticated even by today's standards.

[pages 158–159]

The Auburn Automobile Company dates back to 1902, when American carriage builders Frank and Morris Eckhart began experimenting with motorcars. After a string of moderately successful models, the company fell on hard times, but in 1924 Errett Lobban Cord rescued Auburn from extinction. Cord sold the remaining inventory by repainting the cars in striking two-tone combinations, raising enough cash to keep the company viable and to hire James Crawford to design the next generation of Auburn cars.

1928 AUBURN 8-115 SPEEDSTER

The "Boat-Tail" Speedster further enhanced Auburn's growing reputation. Its body was styled by renowned industrial designer Count Alexis de Sakhnoffsky, known for his Emerson "Mae West" radios, streamlined trucks, and 1937 Mercury Bicycle. But the car was more than just elegant; its straight-8-cylinder

Lycoming engine also generated 115 horsepower, giving the Speedster the power needed to race against its archrival, Stutz.

[pages 78–79]

1934 AUBURN MODEL 12-160 SALON

Although the stock market crash of 1929 initially hurt sales, Auburn rebounded nicely, selling more than 28,000 cars in 1931. The following year, the company introduced its V12 model—further evidence of its desire to move upmarket. But in the uncertain economy, sales slipped again, and only 7,700 cars were produced in 1934.

[pages 34, 72–73]

1935 AUBURN 851 SPEEDSTER

The most famous of all Auburns, the two-passenger, supercharged Boat-Tail Speedster nearly saved the company in 1935. Gordon Buehrig brought it to life, penning a long, low hood, steeply raked V-windshield, chrome pipes, voluptuous pontoon fenders, and a dramatic tapered tail. The signature of either Ab Jenkins or Wade Morton, both famous racecar drivers, was displayed on a small dashboard plaque that certified the car's triple-digit test run. But it was not enough to keep Auburn afloat, and although a 1937 model was planned, 1936 proved to be the foundering marque's final year.

[pages 22, 80–81, 82–83, 84, 85]

BENTLEY
England

BMW
(Bayerische Motoren Werke)
Germany

Walter Owen "W. O." Bentley—originally an importer of European cars—announced his first car, a 3-litre prototype, in May 1919. The car was delivered in 1921, and the following year the "Bentley Boys" began racing. These well-heeled British gentleman-racers won the first Le Mans in 1924 with a Bentley 3-Litre and had consecutive victories from 1927 through 1930. Despite success on the racetrack, however, W. O.'s company was always underfunded. Bentley was acquired by Rolls-Royce in 1931, and the two companies remained together until January 2003.

1927 BENTLEY 3-LITRE

The car that built Bentley's reputation, the 3-Litre, featured a 4-cylinder, four-valves-per-cylinder engine, with an overhead camshaft and four-speed transmission. The coach-work was by Chalmer and Hoyer of England.
[page 136]

1929 BENTLEY 4 1/2-LITRE
HARRISON TOURER

J. H. Hanley and R. H. Dutton brought this Bentley, pictured above, to the United States to set a transcontinental speed record in 1929. Starting from New York, the drivers reached Chicago in record time. But before continuing on their westward journey, they were held at gunpoint by two burly men who convinced them not to set an American record in a British car. Hanley and Dutton never completed the attempt.
[pages 132–133, 134–135, 137]

1934 BENTLEY 3 1/2-LITRE
FIXED HEAD SALOON
by Freestone & Webb

V. E. Freestone and A. J. Webb formed their coach-building company in 1923, adhering to the highest standards of quality and materials.

Freestone & Webb proved to be Bentley's most popular bodies; in fact, 230 bodies were ordered for Bentley's 3-Litre model.
[page 142]

1937 BENTLEY 4 1/4-LITRE
GURNEY NUTTING
SEDANCA COUPÉ

In the early 1900s, automobile bodies were built with wooden framework. So it was only natural that carpenter J. Gurney Nutting open his own firm in 1919 to create custom car bodies. His company, Gurney Nutting, featured the talents of stylist A. E. "Mac" McNeil and held the Royal Warrant, which allowed it to produce coachwork for Prince Edward of Wales, the duke of York, and other members of the royal family.
[pages 131, 140–141]

Long before BMW began building great sporting cars, it produced engines for aircraft, motorboats, lorries, and motorcycles. The marque's first car, the BMW Dixi, was a version of the Austin Seven produced under license in 1928. BMW's first 6-cylinder car, the 303, debuted five years later. This series introduced the company's trademark kidney-shaped grille, and featured rack and pinion steering and hydraulic brakes.

1937 BMW 327
CABRIOLET

The early BMWs progressed in size, power, and performance. The 327, available as both a coupé and a convertible, looked to its predecessor for inspiration. Its engine was based on the previous 326 model, which created 50 horsepower from a 2-litre capacity.
[page 182]

1938 BMW 328

The lightweight 328 roadster was BMW's most significant effort of the 1930s. The car featured an 80-horsepower engine with hemispherical combustion chambers and cross pushrods. Its body contained headlights that were partially faired into the front fenders, and its rear continued the aerodynamic theme with enclosed rear wheels and a sloping tail. As a sports-racer, the 328 was successful its first time out and went on to win more than one hundred races between 1936 and 1939.
[page 183]

*Like many other manu-
facturers, Brewster had
its roots in carriage building, dating back to 1810.
Then in 1926, Rolls-
Royce began to build its
cars in Springfield,
Massachusetts, and
acquired Brewster to
produce its bodies. The
partnership was short-
lived, though, and in 1934
Rolls-Royce ended its
American efforts and
consolidated automobile
production in England.*

*Meanwhile, Brewster
continued its operations
in North America. During
the Great Depression,
former president of Rolls-
Royce of America John
Inskip saw a need for
elegant cars that would
not flaunt their owners'
wealth. So he continued
to produce beautiful but
conservative Brewster
bodies and made them
available with chassis
from Ford, Buick, Cadillac,
Packard, and Lincoln.*

1935 BREWSTER
TOWN CAR (FORD V-8)

The 1934–1935
Brewsters, such as the
models pictured above,
were renowned for their
unique grilles and
bumpers. At first glance
the grille appears heart
shaped, but many car afi-
cionados believe that the
tip of a fountain pen
served as the grille's true
inspiration.
[pages 64–65]

*The name Bugatti evokes
romantic images of dash-
ing sports-racers and
elegant touring cars—a
reflection of its talented
creator, Ettore Bugatti.
Trained in the fine arts in
his native Milan, the
young Ettore eschewed
the influence of his artist
father, Carlo, and moved
to Germany to practice
the mechanical arts.
Despite his rebellious
attitude, he often used
classical proportions and
shapes in his designs, even
carrying these trends into
the engine compartment
and its internal workings.*

*Interestingly, Bugatti
numbered his elegant
designs. Ever resourceful,
he built his own car—the
Type 10—in his cellar
while he worked for other
manufacturers. By 1909,
he was able to move into
his own facility at
Molsheim in Alsace (the
German territory that
would become part of
France after World War
I), where he continued to
improve on his initial
designs. The following
year, the marque's first
cars—the Type 13S—were
delivered to customers,
and in 1911 Bugatti's
660-pound shaft-driven
4-cylinder car took
second place in the French
Grand Prix. By 1914
the trademark horseshoe
radiator had appeared,
and an incredible legacy
had begun.*

1927 BUGATTI TYPE 38A

The Type 38A appeared
only in the years 1926 and
1927. Lavocat & Marsaud
designed the four-passen-
ger body, which housed a
supercharged 8-cylinder,
2-litre engine.
[page 209]

1937 BUGATTI TYPE 57S
ATALANTE

The Type 57 chassis lent
itself to some of the
greatest automobiles ever
designed. Ettore's son
Jean had the distinction
of styling these grand
touring cars, including the
fabulous Atalante.
Bugatti's Type 57S rode
on a 117.5-inch wheel-
base with a straight-
8-cylinder engine that
produced over 170
horsepower and a 95-
mile-per-hour top speed.
[pages 200–201, 202, 203,
204, 205, 270]

1938 BUGATTI TYPE 57SC
ATLANTIC COUPÉ

Jean Bugatti created the
Atlantic prototype, which
was built from Elektron,
an aluminum-magnesium
alloy that was unweldable
and required riveted
construction. Only two
cars were ever produced.
Even though these cars
were made of weldable
aluminum, Bugatti chose
to retain the original dramatic riveted flanges on
the body and fenders.
Helicopter-style doors
swept into the roof and
opened to create a series
of graceful curves that
welcomed driver and pas-
senger into the elegant
interior. The Atlantic
Coupé has earned great
fame as one of the most
beautiful cars in the
world, winning Best of
Show at the prestigious
Pebble Beach Concours
d'Elegance in 1990.
[pages 224–225, 226–227, 228,
229, 230, 231, 232, 233,
234–235]

In 1902, while Henry Ford was busy building racecars, the directors of the Henry Ford Company asked Henry M. Leland for assistance in liquidating their firm. Leland, a well-known engineer with a background in precision machining, instead chose to reorganize the company. He renamed it after Antoine de la Mothe Cadillac, the French explorer who discovered Detroit two hundred years earlier—and the Cadillac Automobile Company immediately started production with engines of Leland's design. With that, Henry Ford left to form Ford Motor Company, and two great American automobile companies were born.

Leland built his cars with precise tolerances. In 1908 he ran a standardization test in Great Britain, where three of his 1-cylinder engines were dissembled, their parts mixed and then reassembled. All three ran perfectly. For this feat, Cadillac was awarded the Royal Automobile Club's Dewar Trophy, and the company proudly adopted the slogan, "The Standard of the World." The following

year, Cadillac was thrust into greater prominence when it was purchased by William C. Durant, who combined the company with Olds, Oakland, and Buick to form General Motors.

1928 CADILLAC 341A
DUAL COWL SPORT
PHAETON

The year 1928 saw the first Cadillacs designed by General Motors's new styling chief, Harley Earl. The cars, similar to Earl's 1927 LaSalle, were available in magnificent color combinations. This new direction was expressed in General Motors's sales literature, "Color Creations from Nature's Studios," which stated, "[Cars] should be colored as Nature paints—with a mastery based alike on appreciation of artistic values and knowledge of the science of color."
[pages 24, 98]

1936 CADILLAC V16
FLEETWOOD
SPECIAL ROADSTER

As the Great Depression began to dent sales of expensive, multicylinder (12 and 16-cylinder) cars, Cadillac looked for ways to make its V16 more attractive to buyers. To that end Cadillac made three special models with Fleetwood bodies—a four-door sports phaeton, a parade car, and a special roadster. Of these custom variations, just one Special Roadster, pictured here, was created.
[pages 94–95, 96, 97]

1937 CADILLAC V16
FLEETWOOD

Just a few short years after it was introduced in 1930, the luster of the V16 began to wear off. Advancing technology was making smaller V8 engines less expensive—

and more attractive. As a result, only fifty V16s were built in 1937; of those, just four were stationary coupés. Each weighed over six thousand pounds on a massive 154-inch wheelbase.
[pages 92–93, 101, 102–103]

1947 CADILLAC SERIES 62
CONVERTIBLE COUPÉ

From 1942 to 1945 Cadillac's resources were directed toward the war effort, producing light tanks and components. New styles had to wait until 1948 so that a backlog of 100,000 orders could be filled as quickly as possible. In 1947, eleven models based on prewar designs were available. A remarkable 62,000 units were sold, 6,755 of which were convertibles. All were powered by Cadillac's 346-cubic-inch V8, generating 150 horsepower.
[pages 23, 99, 104–105, 106–107]

Walter P. Chrysler had worked with Buick, Willys Overland, and Maxwell-Chalmers for years before he founded Chrysler Corporation in 1924. Blessed with a keen business acumen, Chrysler introduced his well-built, reasonably priced car to the market at precisely the right time, acquired Dodge, created DeSoto and Plymouth, and in less than five years turned Chrysler Corporation into a major automaker.

1932 CHRYSLER IMPERIAL
SPEEDSTER
by LeBaron

This Imperial Speedster was restyled at LeBaron to meet customer demand for a more dashing roadster. Among other changes, LeBaron removed the running boards to allow for dramatic fenders and raked the windshield more steeply.
[pages 60, 61]

CORD
The United States

DELAGE
France

1932 CHRYSLER IMPERIAL
SPEEDSTER CH

This custom speedster was Walter P. Chrysler's personal car. Based on the shorter 135-inch CH wheelbase, it featured storage compartments in the front fenders, quad horns, and a fire engine red interior!

[pages 109, 110, 111]

1948 CHRYSLER
TOWN AND COUNTRY

The postwar Chryslers were generally reissues of early 1940s cars. The white ash and wood panels provided structural support, while the leather interior and Highlander wool gave it a distinctive, country feel.

[page 108]

E. L. Cord was already well known when he created a line of cars to fit between his affordable Auburns and high-priced Duesenbergs. The Cord, which showcased advanced front-wheel-drive technology and dramatic styling, solidified E. L. Cord's reputation as one of the great automobile makers of his generation.

1931 CORD L-29

The L-29 was introduced to wide acclaim in 1929. Its front-wheel drive enabled the car to sit lower on its chassis, allowing for a beautiful, flowing line usually reserved for the great European marques.

[page 25]

1936 CORD 810

Gordon Buehrig designed the landmark 810 in 1935. Years ahead of its time in styling, the 810 featured front-wheel drive, headlights enclosed in the front fenders, a steeply raked windshield, and no running boards. Its most unusual feature was the "coffin nose"—horizontal slats that surrounded the front of the car. With the 810 the automobile had truly shed its horse-and-buggy roots.

[pages 76, 77]

1937 CORD 812
SPORTSMAN

The addition of a supercharger increased the 810's horsepower rating—the 812's predecessor—from 125 to 190. But slow sales resulting from manufacturing problems doomed the 810/812 series, as well as E. L. Cord's other automotive adventures.

[pages 74–75]

Automobiles Delage dates back to 1905, when founder Louis Delage introduced his first car at the Paris Salon. Like many others at that time, this car was a conglomeration of parts from other manufacturers. So to stand out from the crowd, Delage chose to race his cars. He found success early, and with the notoriety he gained from racing and profits from World War I military contracts, Delage began building luxury cars to compete against Hispano-Suiza. These custom-body automobiles were some of France's most dramatic coach-built cars.

1932 DELAGE D8-SS
SPEEDSTER
by Letourneur et Marchand

Dashing in shape, striking in color, this purple speedster is one of only two built. The custom body was created by Letourneur et Marchand and powered by a 4-litre, 145-horsepower engine capable of speeds up to 100 miles per hour.

[page 221]

1932 DELAGE D8-SS
by Fernandez & Darrin

Fernandez & Darrin was one of the many great French coachbuilders who worked with the D8 chassis. The D8 was striking for its contrasts: A longtime Grand Prix winner with a reputation for high-powered performance, the car also exuded luxury, with lavish Lalique crystal adorning its radiator.

[pages 190, 191]

1938 DELAGE D8-120 SS
by deVillars

This speedster was introduced in 1938 at the last prewar salon in Paris. Its riveted-seam style was reminiscent of the Bugatti Type 57SC Atlantic Coupé. Its elegant design embodied a popular axiom of the time: "A gentleman drives an Alfa Romeo, is driven in a Rolls-Royce, but buys his mistress a Delage."

[pages 206–207, 208]

DELAHAYE
France

DU PONT
The United States

DUBONNET
France

Emile Delahaye began designing and building gasoline-powered engines in the early 1880s. Within a few years he had built an entire car, and in 1895 he obtained a French patent. As did most builders of his day, Delahaye also raced his invention.

Delahaye retired from the auto business in 1901, but the marque continued building a variety of cars under new ownership—also producing delivery trucks, fire trucks, and marine engines in great numbers. After World War I, the firm faced increased competition from lower-priced manufacturers. This led to another change in ownership and an eventual merge with Delage. But the marque never lost its edge; in 1934 Delahaye returned to racing and found immediate success with its new Type 135.

1937 DELAHAYE 135M
by Figoni et Falaschi

This "teardrop coupé" was as potent as it was beautiful. The 3.5-litre, 6-cylinder engine was rated at 140 horsepower, and with its unique four-speed electromagnetic transmission, the car could reach speeds of 125 miles per hour.
[pages 186–187, 188–189]

1947 DELAHAYE 135M
FRANAY CABRIOLET

Delahaye continued to build cars of prewar design until 1947. Its chassis, however, were still well made and worthy of beautiful coachwork. In fact, the Franay Cabriolet pictured above won first prize at the first postwar Paris Auto Show, where it was purchased by Prince Rainier of Monaco.
[pages 192–193]

1947 DELAHAYE 135MS
ROADSTER
by Henri Chapron

French designer Henri Chapron gave the 135MS a modern postwar look, yet retained some classical forms from the 1930s, such as winged details and wire wheels.
[page 220]

1947 DELAHAYE 135MS
by Figoni et Falaschi

Joseph Figoni and Ovidio Falaschi were known for their outlandish designs. Their Figoni et Falaschi Delahaye was instantly recognizable for its long, flowing shape, and its wheels were often encased in bodywork to complete the theme. The car pictured above was reputedly commissioned by the Aga Khan. Years later, his son Ali Khan gave the red two-seater to movie legend Rita Hayworth.
[pages 194–195, 196, 197, 198–199]

E. Paul du Pont began building cars in 1920, having engaged in the marine engine business during World War I. His new company, Du Pont Motors, Inc., was a private venture—unconnected to the family's E. I. Du Pont de Nemours & Co. Du Pont Motors lasted more than twelve years, and during that period the manufacturer built a total of 537 vehicles, including speedsters, roadsters, saloons, and phaetons, with bodies by Merrimac, Derham, Waterhouse, and Murphy.

1931 DU PONT MODEL H

Du Pont, like many of its competitors, was not able to fight off the effects of the Great Depression. This Model H—an elegant black-and-white touring car that appeared at the New York Auto Show in 1931—was a glorious postscript to the marque. It was the only Open Dual Cowl model of the three Model H cars built, and the only one that survives today.
[pages 26–27]

Andre Dubonnet, aperitif heir, was a racecar driver and automotive engineer. In the mid-1930s, he purchased a few Hispano-Suiza chassis to showcase his independent suspensions to automobile manufacturers in Europe and in the United States. When these bare-chassis had served their purpose, Dubonnet asked the renowned Jacques Saoutchik to design and build the Xenia for his personal use and possible speed-record attempts.

1937 DUBONNET
HISPANO H-6C XENIA
by Saoutchik

Jacques Saoutchik, a Russian cabinetmaker by trade, was known for the flamboyant coachwork created in his Paris studios, and his lavishly designed Dubonnet Hispano H-6C did not disappoint. The airplane canopy greenhouse, sliding doors, sweeping fenders, and uplifted tail all contributed to its breathtaking—but still radical—design.
[pages 236–237, 238–239, 240, 241, 242, 243, 244–245, 246]

DUESENBERG
The United States

FRANKLIN
The United States

HISPANO-SUIZA
France

Frederick "Fred" and August "Augie" Duesenberg immigrated to Iowa from Lippe, Germany, in 1884. The brothers began their career repairing farm equipment and building bicycles. Within a few years, however, they moved on to designing car engines, and in 1919 they moved to Newark, New Jersey, and founded F. S. and A. S. Duesenberg Motors. The Duesenbergs built some of the world's finest racecar engines, winning the French Grand Prix in 1921 and the Indianapolis 500 three times in the 1920s. But their efforts to build road cars proved financially unsound. Hoping to restore the company to financial health, automotive tycoon E. L. Cord bought Duesenberg in 1926 and gave Fred creative license to design the best car money could buy. But their union was short-lived: By 1937 the Great Depression and slow recovery forced the end of operations.

1931 DUESENBERG
MODEL SJ "FRENCH
SPEEDSTER"
by Figoni et Falaschi

The "French Speedster" is considered by many to be the most graceful of all Duesenbergs. Coachbuilder Joseph Figoni built the boat-tail speedster of aluminum for Duesenberg's Paris dealer, E. Z. Sadovich. The supercharged 6.9-litre, straight-8-cylinder engine produced 320 horsepower, achieving 100 miles per hour from a standing start in just seventeen seconds.
[pages 43, 44–45, 46–47, 50, 51]

1935 DUESENBERG
MODEL J WALKER
LEGRAND CONVERTIBLE
COUPÉ

The Walker LeGrand was designed by Herb Newport and built in a series of three. It featured such advancements as dual overhead camshafts, four valves per cylinder, automatic chassis lubrication, and adjustable four-wheel brakes.
[pages 35, 52–53]

1935 DUESENBERG
MODEL SJ
by Bohman & Schwartz

Bohman & Schwartz of Pasadena, California, built a number of custom bodies for the Model J Duesenberg chassis, including land-speed record-holder Ab Jenkins's "Mormon Meteor."
[page 48]

1935 DUESENBERG
MODEL SJ CONVERTIBLE
VICTORIA
by Graber

E. L. Cord wanted the Duesenberg to compete with Europe's best. To that end, each of the 481 chassis was designed for custom coachwork. Graber, of Switzerland, was one of a handful of European coachbuilders who took on this task. "It's a Duesey!" was an expression used to describe anything in a class by itself—and the Model J and SJ Duesenbergs truly were.
[page 49]

The Franklin was the world's best-known air-cooled car—and with elliptical springing and old-fashioned wooden chassis, it was an anomaly. To prove the reliability of air cooling, L. L. Whitman drove a 1904 Franklin from New York to San Francisco in just thirty-three days, almost half the time of the previous record. Yet though the car was reliable, without a traditional radiator in front it was not exactly elegant. In 1925 noted designer Frank De Causse was hired at the urging of disgruntled dealers who felt the car's unusual styling was hurting sales. De Causse—and later Raymond Dietrich—went on to design beautiful broughams, speedsters, and sedans. Their designs increased Franklin sales to a peak of 14,000 cars in 1929, but it was not enough. The company folded in 1934.

1930 FRANKLIN SERIES
147 SPORT RUNABOUT

Famed aviator Charles Lindbergh was a Franklin devotee. To capitalize on Lindbergh's notoriety, H. H. Franklin used an airplane as the company's mascot, perched above the ornamental radiator shell.
[pages 16, 66–67]

While still in his early twenties, Swiss engineer Marc Birkigt designed the Castro—the first offering of the Barcelona-based Hispano-Suiza. Birkigt went on to become one of the great engine designers of his day, creating 2-, 4-, and 6-cylinder automobile engines and the famous A8 airplane engine for the Spanish and French governments. Birkigt moved to Paris in 1910, which allowed Hispano to capitalize on the wealthier French market. There, Hispano-Suiza became the principal transport for Europe's elite, designing cars such as the King Alfonso XIII and the fabulous H6.

1928 HISPANO-SUIZA
H-6C

Hispano-Suiza's aircraft-engine heritage led to the car's famous stork mascot, which pays homage to the French fighter pilots of World War I.
[page 222]

In 1900, after managing the Benz factory in Mannheim for three years, August Horch left and founded A. Horch & Co. His cars were known for their engineering excellence but were still priced below competing Mercedes-Benz models. After a series of internal disputes, Horch left his company and formed Audi, which, ironically, eventually merged with Horch, DKW, and Wanderer to form Auto Union. Their interlocking four-ring emblem is still used by Audi, the last remaining member of this once-great automobile conglomerate.

1939 HORCH 853A CABRIOLET

The big 853 was similar in style and feel to the Mercedes-Benz 540K Cabriolet A—but Horch outsold its competitor by more than two to one. Yet the Horch was heavy—over 5,300 pounds—and its performance suffered. Automobile production did not resume after World War II.

[pages 180–181]

Cesare Isotta and Vincenzo Fraschini went into partnership in 1898, importing French cars into Italy. Soon after, they began creating cars, heavy vehicles, and aero engines under their own name. In 1905 Isotta-Fraschini brought Giustino Cattaneo to the company, where he remained chief designer until 1933. Cattaneo's designs found favor on both sides of the Atlantic—Fleetwood, LeBaron, and Castagna alike supplied grand bodies for the expensive $9,000 chassis.

1930 ISOTTA-FRASCHINI MODEL 8-A
by Castagna

Prior to World War I, Isotta-Fraschini marketed fifty different models of cars. Their focus changed after the war, however, and they released only one model in 1919: the Tipo 8. This car was intended to compete with the best cars in Europe and the United States. Film star Rudolph Valentino was often loaned a car for publicity purposes, but he died before taking possession of his own Fleetwood-bodied roadster.

[pages 8, 155, 160]

Jaguar Cars, Ltd., started out as the Swallow Sidecar Company of Blackpool, England. The company began by building motorcycle sidecars, but in 1928, after five years of production, company founder William Lyons and his partner William Walmsley extended their product line to include sporting bodies for popular European cars, such as Austin, Morris, Fiat, Swift, and Standard. Their first sports car, the SS-90, was introduced in 1935, and the following year their four-door Jaguar Saloon made its appearance. The cars were a success, and William Lyons went on to become one of England's most revered automotive designers, creating the legendary XK-series of the 1950s. For this he was knighted "Sir William" in 1956.

1948 JAGUAR 3 1/2-LITRE SALOON

After 1945 the company renamed its cars Jaguars; the "SS" initials—which denoted the Swallow Sidecar Company—had become tainted by the war. That, however, was one of the only changes. Postwar Saloons, such as the one featured above, were in reality 1940 models with updated mechanicals that retained the elegant prewar styling.

[page 143]

Wisconsin brothers William and George Kissel began their careers making engines and farm equipment in the late nineteenth century. By 1906 the ambitious brothers had produced their first car—the Kissel. Over time, Kissel Kar offered a number of body styles and engine choices, including funeral cars and taxis. But the brothers were struggling financially. In 1930 entrepreneur Archie Andrews contracted with the Kissels to build 1,500 of his Ruxton cars, but the brothers were unable to fulfill the contract. They filed for bankruptcy later that year.

1927 KISSEL 8-75 SPEEDSTER

The 1918 yellow Kissel Speedster—predecessor of the 8-75—was the most talked about car at the New York Show that year. Its radiator shell had a full, round shape that continued all the way to the cowl, giving the "Gold Bug" an unusual, yet beautiful and spare look. Famous entertainer Al Jolson and aviator Amelia Earhart were two of its many devotees.

[pages 20–21]

LALIQUE
France

LASALLE
The United States

LINCOLN
The United States

René Lalique was already a world-famous jeweler when he turned his attention to glassmaking at the age of fifty. Lalique found the automobile alluring and chose to create glass mascots to adorn the radiators of luxurious motorcars. In all, he would create thirty mascots in a variety of subjects—nudes, animals, birds, fish, insects, and even comets. Some were lit with a small lightbulb and colored gels that created a glowing effect at night.

LALIQUE CINQ CHEVAUX

Lalique's first four designs were created from the many perfume bottles and paperweights he had designed as a glassmaker. Then in 1925 André Citroën commissioned Lalique to design a glass mascot specifically for the introduction of the Citroën 5CV. *Cinq Chevaux* is the only Lalique mascot containing multiple figures.
[page 211]

LALIQUE VICTOIRE

Victoire (Spirit of the Wind) appeared on a Minerva at the Paris Motor Salon in 1928. Symbolizing power and speed, this art deco masterpiece is the largest and most famous of Lalique's mascots.
[page 223]

LALIQUE TÊTE DE PAON

The 1928 *Tête de Paon (Peacock's Head)* was heavily detailed and quite tall, standing six inches high. Like many of Lalique's designs, it was available in a variety of colors—turquoise, amethyst-tint, violet, and clear glass.
[page 210]

General Motors president Alfred Sloan wanted to keep up with the trend-setting style of the European marques. So, in 1926 he authorized the creation of the LaSalle as a highly styled companion to General Motors's Cadillac. For this task, Sloan and the president of Cadillac, Lawrence Fisher, called on Harley Earl, a young stylist from southern California. For Earl the assignment was a designer's dream come true. Not only was he able to design the new car, but he was also given command of GM's new styling department—the Art & Colour Section. Earl soon infused new vitality and color into the whole GM line.

1930 LASALLE
7-PASSENGER TOURING CAR
by Fleetwood

Cadillac had stopped offering the touring model in its 1930 lineup, and this Fleetwood-bodied LaSalle filled the void. According to LaSalle's sales brochure, it had "the ample roominess so desirable in an open car" and even boasted "it would be difficult to resist an invitation to drive this spirited car." The car truly embodied "every essential of motoring enjoyment." The LaSalle pictured here is one of only 240 built and was originally purchased by Dorothy Quincy Roosevelt, cousin of President Theodore Roosevelt.
[page 90]

1940 LASALLE SERIES
52 CONVERTIBLE

The U.S. economy improved dramatically near the end of the 1930s, rendering the lower-priced LaSalle unnecessary for General Motors. The decision to discontinue the car was easy; it was made almost entirely of Cadillac components anyway. But the LaSalle had made an impact by bringing style to the fore at General Motors.
[pages 88–89, 91]

Henry M. Leland, founder of Cadillac, left the company in 1917 over a dispute with William Durant, head of General Motors. Their argument centered on Durant's refusal to build Liberty aero engines for the Allies before the United States had fully entered World War I. Ever patriotic, Leland chose to build the aero engines in his own company, which he named for his boyhood hero, Abraham Lincoln. After the war, Leland and his son Wilfrid set their sights on automobiles, producing their first Lincoln in 1920.

The early Lincolns were blessed with strong engineering—equal to that of Cadillac—but were cursed with dull styling. A most unlikely person, however, would change that: Henry Ford. Ford—who twenty years prior had been at odds with Henry Leland—bought the ailing company in 1922 at the request of his son Edsel. Edsel Ford wanted to improve the styling of the Lincoln and thus produce a complement to his father's Model T. Edsel made major style changes and soon began manufacturing elegant Lincolns, such as the Model Ks, Zephyrs, and Continentals.

**1932 LINCOLN KB
MODEL 248 CONVERTIBLE
ROADSTER**
by LeBaron

The KB was introduced in 1932 and allowed Lincoln to compete with the V12s produced by Cadillac, Auburn, Packard, and Pierce-Arrow. Many of the great coachbuilders— Murphy, Dietrich, Brunn, LeBaron—contributed bodies to the 1,515 cars built, 112 of which were convertible roadsters.

[pages 112–113, 114, 115]

1940 LINCOLN CONTINEN-TAL CONVERTIBLE

The Lincoln Continental was designed by E. T. "Bob" Gregorie, who in 1935 created Ford's first styling department. Originally handmade as a one-of-a-kind example for Edsel Ford, the car proved to be one of the automobile industry's greatest designs.

[pages 116–117]

Mercedes-Benz traces its roots to the very first automobiles of Karl Benz and Gottlieb Daimler. Karl Benz built the world's first motorcar propelled by an internal combustion engine in 1885. Working independently, Gottlieb Daimler was not far behind, creating his first car the following year. Their two companies would merge some forty years later to become Mercedes-Benz.

Daimler's cars were given the name "Mercedes" in 1900. That year Emil Jellinek, an Austrian motoring enthusiast, convinced Daimler to build a series of sporting cars to his specifications. Jellinek bought all thirty-six cars and christened them after his eleven-year-old daughter, Mercedes. Gottlieb Daimler, however, never knew his cars by this new name. He died just before the cars were delivered, and the company came under the control of his son, Paul.

The Daimler and Benz companies continued on their separate paths until 1926, when the difficult post–World War I economy necessitated their merger. Although the new firm had been formed out of hardship, Daimler-Benz went on to set standards for engineering excellence for decades to come.

1928 MERCEDES-BENZ S

Brilliant young engineer Ferdinand Porsche designed the "Typ S," the first offering from the new firm. In addition to his work with Mercedes-Benz, Professor Porsche eventually went on to create the Volkswagen and a number of great prewar racecars. Porsche also left behind one of the world's great automotive legacies: His son, Dr. Ferry Porsche, designed the Porsche sports car, which still carries the family name.

[pages 162–163]

1929 MERCEDES-BENZ SSK

In 1929 Mercedes-Benz offered a lighter, shorter version of the S. With the addition of the super-charger, or kompressor, the engine was capable of 250 horsepower. Only thirty-three SSK cars were built in its four years of production.

[page 170]

1930 MERCEDES-BENZ SSK "COUNT TROSSI"

Count Carlo Felice Trossi was a well-known motoring enthusiast who drove for the Scuderia Ferrari race team. According to his family, the count purchased the SSK as a running chassis, sketched its beautiful design, and then had it built in England. His one-off design was awarded Best of Show at the 1993 Pebble Beach Concours d'Elegance.

[pages 164–165, 166–167, 168, 169, 177]

**1937 MERCEDES-BENZ
540 K SPECIAL ROADSTER**

The 540 K was introduced in 1936. Its two-ton chassis was available with a variety of body styles, including the limited edition Special Roadster, pictured above. This car was displayed by Mercedes-Benz at the 1937 Berlin Motor Show. Sixty years later it won Best of Show at the famed Amelia Island Concours d'Elegance.

[pages 170, 171, 174–175, 176]

**1938 MERCEDES-BENZ
540 K CABRIOLET A**

Mercedes's in-house coachbuilder, Sindelfingen, created the 540 K. There were no standard colors; customers could choose their own combinations. Just eighty-three Cabriolet A cars were built until the series ended in 1939.

[pages 172–173, 178–179]

The marque may not be well known, but the Minerva was a wonderful, well-built car. The company was founded in Antwerp, Belgium, by Sylvain de Jong, a Dutchman who started out building bicycles in 1897. A few years later he began producing cars, reaching a peak of 3,000 in 1913. But like many of Europe's small automotive marques, Minerva's manufacturing was disrupted by World War I, and by the late 1930s its motorcar production had ended. During and after World War II, the firm managed to stay afloat by continuing limited production of commercial and off-road vehicles, but in 1957 Minerva finally closed its doors.

1927 MINERVA AK
by LeBaron

The Minerva was used by a number of royal European households. The kings of Belgium, Norway, and Sweden all owned Minervas—as did the king of America's automobile industry, Henry Ford. In 1927 Minerva introduced its AK model. It featured a 5.9-litre, 6-cylinder engine, majestic 149.5-inch wheelbase, and four-wheel brakes. An imposing car, it was distinguished by its V-type windshield, long cowl, and mascot, the Goddess of Automobiles, which perched upon its radiator.

[pages 150–151, 152, 153, 154]

Packard was born out of a desire for excellence. In 1899 cofounder James Packard decided he wanted to build the best car available—one that was even better than a Winton. To that end James and his brother William used their industrial manufacturing facilities in Warren, Ohio, to produce 1-, 2-, and 4-cylinder automobiles. Henry Joy joined the brothers in 1902 and moved the firm to Detroit the following year, but Packard's quest for quality never changed. The company stood proudly behind its slogan, "Ask the man who owns one." The statement asserted, in effect, that every Packard owner was a happy one, which was largely true. Packard remained a major manufacturer of high-quality cars for almost sixty years.

1926 PACKARD MODEL 326 ROADSTER

This 6-cylinder series was introduced in 1925 and built until 1928. The engine produced 60 horsepower and rode on a 126-inch wheelbase. "The

Arts and Crafts of Packard," the sales literature of the time, stated, "Into all its bodies are built the expressions of artists and artisans that make them worthy to be identified as products of the Packard fine name."

[page 36]

1930 PACKARD 745 CONVERTIBLE COUPÉ
by Derham

In 1926 Packard started making custom coachwork available as part of its product line. Renowned automotive coachbuilders, such as Fleetwood, Derham, and Dietrich, produced bodies for Packard's Original Creations by Master Designers. The handsome 8-cylinder, seventh-series Convertible Coupé pictured above is only one of two known examples produced by the Derham Body Company of Rosemont, Pennsylvania.

[pages 28–29, 31]

1934 PACKARD 1104
DUAL COWL PHAETON

Packard made a variety of 8- and 12-cylinder models during 1934. Wheelbases varied from 129.5 inches to a comfortable 147 inches. Four-, five-, and seven-passenger vehicles were made in both standard and custom configurations. Of the thirty-three Dual Cowl Phaetons ever produced, eleven still exist.

[page 30]

1934 PACKARD 1108
SPORT PHAETON
by LeBaron

Packard's product range was broad, and so was their pricing. For instance, 1934 Standard 8-cylinder cars started at $2,350, while custom LeBarons cost more than three times as much.

[page 32]

PACKARD
Continued

PIERCE-ARROW
The United States

ROLLS-ROYCE
England

1934 PACKARD 1104
CONVERTIBLE VICTORIA

The 142-inch wheelbase,
eleventh-series Packard
was available in eleven
different body configura-
tions. Its engine was a
straight-8-cylinder with
145 horsepower.
[page 37]

1942 PACKARD SUPER-8
180 DARRIN CONVERTIBLE
VICTORIA

Among the most stylish of
all Packards, the Darrin
was conceived in 1939 by
Howard "Dutch" Darrin,
for his Hollywood clien-
tele. Its cut-down doors,
simple lines, and absence
of running boards were
daring—an indicator of
the styling changes that
would sweep the automo-
bile industry after the war.
Ironically, when produc-
tion resumed in 1946,
Packard chose not to con-
tinue building upscale
cars, leaving Cadillac to
fill that void.
[page 33]

*Founded in Buffalo, New
York, in 1855, Pierce-
Arrow had its start pro-
ducing everything from
iceboxes to bicycles. But
it was not until 1901,
after almost fifty years of
operation, that company
treasurer Colonel Charles
Clifton convinced his
employer, George Norman
Pierce, to enter the automobile business. Building
cars brought the company
immediate success. Pierce-
Arrow turned out its first
automobile and was soon
lauded as one of the
"Three Ps" of the indus-
try, joining the ranks of
automotive heavyweights
Peerless and Packard.
Presidents Wilson,
Harding, and Coolidge all
owned Pierce-Arrows.
Pierce-Arrow's glory
faded fast, though:
Throughout the 1920s,
the firm still clung to its
venerable 6-cylinder
engine while its competi-
tors moved on to 8-, 12-,
and even 16-cylinder
power. To stay solvent,
Pierce-Arrow was forced
to merge with Studebaker.
But Studebaker itself*

declared bankruptcy in
1933, and a new financial
group took over. Sales
continued to drop, and
after producing just 167
cars in 1937, Pierce-
Arrow closed its doors
for good.

1933 PIERCE-ARROW 1242
CONVERTIBLE COUPÉ

In 1932 Pierce-Arrow
came out with its first
12-cylinder car in an
attempt to compete with
the multicylinder cars
from Cadillac and
Packard. These cars, such
as the one pictured above,
were available in numer-
ous body styles on three
chassis lengths. The
engines produced either
140 or 150 horsepower
with an increase to 175
horsepower in 1933.
Famous racecar driver
Ab Jenkins drove a
streamlined Pierce-Arrow
to an amazing 127-miles-
per-hour average over a
full twenty-four-hour
period in 1933.
[pages 38–39, 40–41, 42]

*Henry Royce had just fin-
ished building his first car,
the Royce, when he was
introduced to the
Honourable Charles
Stewart Rolls, a wealthy
automobile enthusiast.
Their 1904 introduction
marked the beginning of a
fruitful partnership. Over
the next 100 years, the
name Rolls-Royce would
come to signify a standard
of excellence described as,
simply, "the best." Royce,
a brilliant engineer, earned
that reputation for the
company. On a never-
ending quest for improve-
ment, Rolls-Royce entered
numerous races and
reliability tests. It paid
off: The marque's most
famous series was dubbed
the Silver Ghost because
of its remarkably quiet
and smooth engine—a
marked contrast from the
noisy and unreliable cars
of its day. In production
from 1907 to 1926,
the Silver Ghost set an
unparalleled standard
of excellence that was
later continued by the
Phantom series.*

1927 ROLLS-ROYCE
PHANTOM I BROUGHAM
by Charles Clark & Sons of
Wolverhampton

This elegant Phantom
was created as a birthday
present for the heiress of
the Woolworth fortune.
The coachwork, by
Charles Clark & Sons of
Wolverhampton, featured
sterling silver carriage
lamps and interior details
in twenty-four-karat gold.
The inside even contained
intricate murals on the
ceiling and wood-inlaid
scenes on the passenger
compartment doors.
[pages 122, 123]

1931 ROLLS-ROYCE
PHANTOM I REGENT
by Brewster

The Phantom I was first
introduced in 1925. Its
chassis was similar to the
Silver Ghost but the
Phantom's 6-cylinder,
7.7-litre engine was a
remarkable improvement
over its predecessor's. The
car pictured above was

built by American Rolls-
Royce in Springfield,
Massachusetts. Its body
was built by in-house
coachbuilder, Brewster.
[pages 120–121, 130, 146]

**1931 ROLLS-ROYCE
PHANTOM II CONTINENTAL
CLOSE COUPLED 4-SOME**
by Mulliner

First offered in September
1929, the Phantom II con-
tinued the Rolls-Royce
quest for excellence with
improvements in the
engine—a redesigned
combustion chamber and
manifold—and chassis. By
simplifying and lowering
the chassis, the company
could now offer more
sporting coachwork as an
alternative to its stately
counterpart models.
[page 126]

**1931 ROLLS-ROYCE
PHANTOM II NEWMARKET**
by Brewster

Until 1934, Brewster con-
tinued to make elegant
bodies for Rolls-Royce

chassis manufactured
in the United States.
Production then moved to
Derby, England, where it
remained until moving to
Crewe, Cheshire, in 1946.
[pages 124–125, 138, 139, 147]

**1932 ROLLS-ROYCE
PHANTOM II CONTINENTAL
SPORTS SALOON**
by Mulliner

The Continental was the
most sporting of the
Phantom II cars. It came
with a tuned engine and
high-ratio axle to allow
for speeds up to ninety
miles per hour. The
Phantom II series was
the last design completed
by Henry Royce, who
died in 1938.
[page 128]

**1934 ROLLS-ROYCE 20/25
SHOOTING BRAKE**
by Joseph Cockshoot

As the Silver Ghost
became increasingly
expensive, Rolls-Royce
introduced a slightly

smaller engine/chassis
combination in 1922.
Unlike the larger cars
with their custom coach-
work, the 20/25 series
was available with a standard body. The Shooting
Brake, by coachbuilder
Joseph Cockshoot, was
used primarily for hunting
on English country estates.
[page 127]

**1936 ROLLS-ROYCE
PHANTOM III COUPÉ**
by Barker

The Phantom series
culminated with the
marque's only 12-cylinder
engine, featured in the
Phantom III of 1935–1939.
This powerful V12
borrowed heavily from
Rolls-Royce's experience
in building airplane
engines. But production
on the Phantom III was
cut short by the outbreak
of war in 1939; only 710
cars were produced.
[page 129]

*The Ruxton and its
competitor, the L-29
Cord, were the only front-
wheel-drive automobiles
available in 1929. The
Cord preceded the
Ruxton by a few months,
and was ultimately the
more successful of the
two—which probably
came as no shock to those
familiar with the Ruxton's
unstable beginnings.
The Ruxton was the
brainchild of Archie
Andrews, founder of New
Era Motors. With the help
of several investors—
William Ruxton among
them—Andrews brought
to market his dream front-
wheel-drive car, naming it
after his principal finan-
cier. Unfortunately, before
the car had found its
niche in the marketplace,
Ruxton pulled out of the
deal, as did a number of
other financial supporters.
Andrews lost the funds he
needed to secure a perma-
nent home for his car, and
in 1930, after producing
only 300 Ruxtons, New
Era Motors closed its
doors. Even though the
actual venture—building
the car—was short-lived,
it took an astounding
thirty-six years of litiga-
tion before New Era's
affairs were finally settled.*

1930 RUXTON

The Ruxton's use of
front-wheel drive allowed
for a car that was dramatically lower than most.
The cars were built in a
number of different factories, a reflection of both
the tenuous finances of
New Era Motors and the
stock market crash of
1929. The roadster
pictured above featured
Woodlite headlamps, a
popular option for cars
of the 1920s and 1930s.
[pages 62, 63]

SQUIRE
England

STOUT SCARAB
The United States

STUDEBAKER
The United States

STUTZ
The United States

Englishman Adrian Squire wanted to build the best sports car money could buy. To that end he designed the 1933 Squire. He used only the finest components for his marque, including a unique 110-horsepower Anzani motor, a Rootes supercharger, and bodies by a number of leading coachbuilders. Unfortunately, the flagging economy made survival impossible—just seven of these fine cars were ever built.

1933 SQUIRE
by Van Den Plas

Squire wanted only the best for his car, but it came at a tremendous cost. The price of £1,200 pounds turned out to be double the cost of an Aston Martin and almost equal to that of the famed Bugatti Type 55. Squire simplified the car and reduced the price, but even these drastic measures could not save his dream.
[pages 144–145]

The Stout Scarab was the brainchild of accomplished aeronautical engineer William Stout, well known in aviation for his design of the Ford Tri-motor, a three-engine monoplane. In 1935 Stout turned his attention to automobile design and created the unusual Scarab. The car reflected Stout's desire to provide more interior space compared to the inefficient behemoths of the day. But his ideas, though visionary, proved to be too radical for the public, and only nine examples were built.

1936 STOUT SCARAB

The Scarab was aerodynamic, with a very short sloping hood and a long body that housed a V8 Ford motor in the rear. The interior was even more unusual: Only the driver's seat was stationary. The remaining seats were "occasional" and could be moved to accommodate the passenger's needs. A foldaway card table completed the wicker interior.
[pages 3, 86–87]

Studebaker traces its heritage to 1852, when blacksmiths Henry and Clem Studebaker first built wagons in South Bend, Indiana. The brothers' venture grew to become the largest maker of wagons in the world, allowing them to indulge their interest in automobiles in the late 1890s. In 1902 Studebaker produced an electric car designed by Thomas Edison. Its first gasoline-powered cars were produced the following year.

Albert Erskine became president of the firm in 1916. Under Erskine, Studebaker rose to become one of the largest manufacturers of mass-market cars, building almost 150,000 cars in 1923. Erskine moved Studebaker into the luxury market in 1928 with the introduction of the President Eight and the purchase of Pierce-Arrow. But as the company turned more upscale, the economy began to sag and the Great Depression cut deeply into sales. By 1933 Studebaker was $15 million in debt and Erskine was personally bankrupt. Distraught, he committed suicide after a proposed merger with another manufacturer fell through.

Fortunately, by 1935 Studebaker emerged from its troubles and returned to building more reasonably priced cars. Studebaker acquired Packard in 1954 but could not keep that legendary marque alive. Studebaker ended production ten years later.

1931 STUDEBAKER
PRESIDENT

The President was the top-of-the-line offering from Studebaker. A custom-built racecar version competed at the Indianapolis 500 in 1930.
[pages 70, 71]

1934 STUDEBAKER
COMMANDER COUPÉ

The 1934 Commander received a more stylish, aerodynamic look. The coupé styling was even more daring and was produced in very limited numbers.
[pages 68, 69]

In 1910 Harry C. Stutz opened the Stutz Auto Parts Company to produce a combination rear axle/gearbox. Stutz placed the transmission in a racecar to showcase his invention, and just five weeks later the car finished in eleventh place at the Indianapolis 500. With the publicity, Stutz was flooded with requests to build more cars, and the slogan "The Car That Made Good in a Day" was born. This was the first of many efforts, including the Stutz Bearcat, which became legendary in American racing history.

1928 STUTZ BB
BLACK HAWK SPEEDSTER

Frederick E. Moscovics was brought in to manage the company in 1925, and he started racing its newest models. The Black Hawk Speedsters won wherever they raced and became America's fastest production model—one even reaching 106 miles per hour at Daytona in 1928.
[page 58]

1929 STUTZ CONVERTIBLE
VICTORIA
by Hibbard & Darrin

As the company matured in the 1920s, public demand increased for a car more practical than the bare-bones Bearcat racer or the hell-raising Black Hawk. Stutz responded by making custom bodies available, such as the imposing car pictured above. Thomas L. Hibbard, formerly of LeBaron Carrossiers, and Howard "Dutch" Darrin, built the Convertible Victoria.

[pages 56–57]

1932 STUTZ DV-32
CONVERTIBLE

The last of the marque, the DV-32, had an advanced 32-valve, 8-cylinder engine. It was universally praised but unfortunately, sales were slow. As the Great Depression eroded the upper-echelon automotive market, Stutz found that it could not survive. The company switched from building great cars to building small delivery trucks—a strategy that proved unsuccessful. Stutz declared bankruptcy in 1937.

[pages 54–55, 59, 100]

Talbot-Lago descended from a series of British, French, and Belgian companies, the last of which was Sunbeam-Talbot-Darracq. In 1934 Major Antony Lago rescued Talbot from the failing S.-T.-D. and continued the marque as Tabot-Lago until 1958, when he sold the company to Simca. During Lago's stewardship, Talbot-Lago developed great racing cars that built upon S.-T.-D.'s earlier successes at Le Mans. By 1939 Talbot-Lagos were being made in eleven different body styles, many with coachwork from Figoni et Falaschi.

1938 TALBOT-LAGO T-23
"TEARDROP COUPÉ"
by Figoni et Falaschi

The most beautiful of Tony Lago's cars were the aerodynamic "Teardrop Coupés" designed by Figoni et Falaschi. The car pictured above is the only four-passenger version and features a dramatic sloping roofline, covered rear wheels, and a 4.5-litre engine with Wilson preselect transmission.

[pages 218–219]

Like many other carmakers of the day, Voisin began by building airplanes. In 1907 Gabriel Voisin built and flew the first airplane that took off and landed on its own power. (The Wright airplane needed a catapult for launch.) Voisin made a fortune manufacturing airplanes during World War I, but afterward he turned his facilities to automobile production. These dramatic cars were favored by such rich and famous personalities as architect Le Corbusier, author H. G. Wells, and film stars Maurice Chevalier and Rudolph Valentino.

1925 VOISIN C3L BERLINE
TRANSFORMABLE
by J. Rothschild & Son

This grand touring car had unique "transformable" coachwork, which allowed the rear of the car to open when the roof and its structural supports slid into the body. The rear compartment had beautiful broadcloth upholstery with intricate tapestries on the ceiling and doors. A wine-cooling chamber was even hidden in the floorboards. A popular show car, the Voisin C3L won Best of Show honors at the 2002 Radnor Hunt Concours d'Elegance.

[pages 10, 184–185]

1934 VOISIN C15 ETS
SALIOT ROADSTER

The Roadster pictured above was built by Saliot, who ran a well-known Voisin repair shop. Saliot purchased tooling and parts from the financially ailing Voisin in the early 1930s. The car's beauty is unmistakable; it won Best of Show at Pebble Beach in 2002.

[pages 6, 212, 213, 214–215, 216–217]

SUGGESTED READINGS

Adler, Dennis. *Speed & Luxury: The Great Cars.*
Osceola, Wisconsin: MBI Publishing Company, 1997.

Automobile Quarterly (various editions).

Borgenson, Griffith. *Bugatti by Borgenson: The Dynamics of Mythology.*
London: Osprey, 1981.

Borgenson, Griffith. *Errett Lobban Cord—His Empire, His Motor Cars: Auburn, Cord, Duesenberg.*
Princeton: Automobile Quarterly Publishing, 1984.

Brierley, Brooks. *Auburn, Reo, Franklin and Pierce-Arrow versus Cadillac, Chrylser, Lincoln and Packard.*
Coconut Grove, Florida: Garratt and Stringer, 1991.

Buehrig, Gordon M., and William S. Jackson. *Rolling Sculpture: A Designer and His Work.*
Newfoundland, New Jersey: Haessner, 1975.

Dominguez, Henry. *Edsel Ford and E. T. Gregorie.*
Warrendale, Pennsylvania: Society of Automotive Engineers, 1999.

Georgano, Nick (ed). *The Beaulieu Encyclopedia of the Automobile.*
London: The Stationery Office, 2000.

Kimes, Bevery Rae (ed). *Packard—A History of the Motor Car and the Company.*
Princeton: Automobile Quarterly Publications, 1978.

————. *The Classic Era.*
Des Plaines, Illinois: Classic Car Club of America, 2001.

Kimes, Beverly Rae, with Henry Austin Clark, Jr. *Standard Catalog of American Cars 1805–1942.*
(Third Edition). Iola, Wisconsin: Krause, 1996.

L'Ebe Bugatti: The Bugatti Story.
Philidelphia: Chilton Book Company, 1967.

McCall, Walter M. P. *80 Years of Cadillac LaSalle.*
Minneapolis: Crestline Publishing Company, 1982.

Theberge, Pierre (ed). *Moving Beauty.*
Montreal: The Montreal Museum of Fine Arts, 1995.

Wagner, Rob L. *Classic Cars.*
New York: Friedman/Fairfax Publishers, 2000.

LIST OF OWNERS

I have been fortunate to photograph the greatest cars in the world. Let me take this opportunity to thank the following owners for preserving these wonderful machines:

Auburn-Cord-Duesenberg Museum
Ed and Laurie Ardis
Bernard Berman
Bill Borden
Nicola Bulgari
Joseph Cassini
Ele Chesney
Miles Collier
John Cunningham
John Dennison
Gene and Marlene Epstein
Howard Finkelman
William Ford
The Gallo Collection
Thom and Ginny Gatley
Robert and Grace Gluck
Eldon du Pont Homsey
David Kane
Thomas Kidd
Mark Lankford
Ralph Lauren

Drew Lewis
Bud and Thelma Lyon
Richard Mahoney
Sam and Emily Mann
Dave Markel
Jeff McAllister
Peter and Joanne McManus
John Moir
Charles Morse
José de Pedrosa
Ken Redles
John Rich
Richard Riegel
Ron Schneider
Frederick A. Simeone
Susan Tatios
Noel Thompson
Michael G. Tillson, III
Keith Yost
Elizabeth Zoller
Karl F. Zoller, III

ACKNOWLEDGEMENTS

Motorcars of the Classic Era has been the result of more than twenty years of photography, research, and deep admiration. And yet I could not have accomplished this project without the support of many talented friends, associates, and institutions. Because the cars were photographed in the studio, a large crew of assistants and technicians were necessary to turn my vision into a reality. For this, I am ever grateful to John Burichelli, Esteban Grenados, Bernard Block, and Angelo Gellura of the Hill Studio; and studio assistants Bill Wynes, Dave March, Tom Maher, John Wynn, Misha Kwasniewski, Sophia Wynytski, Ken Burgess, Dan Mezick, Bronwyn Smith, Victoria Satterthwaite, Adam Hoffman, Andy Bausk, Peter Grims, and Eric Furman.

Also, many friends have taken a special interest in my work over the years, helping me to research cars, and transport and access them. I especially need to thank Mike Tillson, Susan Tatios, Ed Tatios, Paul Russell, Janet Oliver, Dave Myers, Mark Lizewskie, Jed Rapoport, Jonathan Stein, David Steinman, and Sandra Zoller. Howard Baker, too, worked hard to keep me focused on this project; I am grateful for his encouragement.

A great many talented artists and designers have worked with me in creating a number of these images. Thank you to Kevin Thompson, Kerry Polite, Bill Beauchamp, Michael Gunselman, Mary Dunham, Kevin Barr, Allen Dugan, John Fetter, and Mark Bofinger.

Thank you to Tehabi Books for believing in this project—Sam Lewis, Eric Pinkham, Chris Capen, and Andrew Arias. Josie Delker and Monika Stout have given the images a wonderful presence, while Betsy Holt, my editor, deserves high praise for deciphering my text. Thanks, too, to the team at Harry N. Abrams—Christopher Sweet, senior editor, and Josh Faught, editorial assistant—for their development and support of this book.

Finally, I am particularly grateful to four special people who have worked tirelessly with me for many years: Lynnette Mager handled the logistics in producing many of these images, taking on that burden so I could concentrate on creating the best photographs possible. Digital artist Dave Phillips made these images better than I could have imagined. Many of these photographs exist only because of his talent, patience, and determination. Merrill Furman helped me write and always encouraged me to express my thoughts. And Robert DePue Brown offered his many years of automotive insight into the research and development of this book—his knowledge and love of cars has been truly inspirational. I am forever indebted to these wonderful people.

TEHABI BOOKS

Tehabi Books developed, designed, and produced *Motorcars of the Classic Era* and has conceived and produced many award-winning books that are recognized for their strong literary and visual content. Tehabi works with national and international publishers, corporations, institutions, and nonprofit groups to identify, develop, and implement comprehensive publishing programs. Tehabi Books is located in San Diego, California. *www.tehabi.com*

President and Publisher Chris Capen
Vice President of Operations Sam Lewis
Director, Corporate Publishing Chris Brimble
Director, Corporate Marketing Marty Remmell
Corporate Sales Manager Andrew Arias
Senior Art Director Josie Delker
Production Artist Monika Stout
Editor Betsy Holt
Copy Editor Jacqueline Garrett
Proofreader Marco Pavia

Tehabi Books offers special discounts for bulk purchases for sales promotions and use as premiums. Specific, large-quantity needs can be met with special editions, custom covers, and by repurposing existing materials. For more information, contact Andrew Arias, Corporate Sales Manager, at Tehabi Books, 4920 Carroll Canyon Road, Suite 200, San Diego, California 92121-3735; or, by telephone, at 800-243-7259.

Photographer and author Michael Furman has been photographing motorcars for over three decades. His portfolio includes an extensive range of automobiles, including one-of-a-kind prototypes, Grand Prix cars, antiques, and sports cars. He is a recognized expert in digital capture and computer-generated imagery, and also a specialist in studio photography, employing elegant lighting and classical design to showcase the quality of these rare and beautiful machines.

Editor Christopher Sweet
Editorial Assistant Josh Faught
Production Manager Kaija Markoe

Library of Congress Cataloging-in-Publication Data

Furman, Michael.
    Motorcars of the classic era / Michael Furman.— 1st ed.
        p. cm.
Includes index.
    ISBN 0-8109-4666-1
    1. Antique and classic cars—Pictorial works. 2. Automobiles—History. I. Title.

    TL15.F87 2003
    629.222'022'2—dc22

                                        2003057896

Published in 2003 by Harry N. Abrams, Incorporated, New York. All rights reserved. No part of the contents of this book may be reproduced without written permission of the publisher.

ISBN 0-8109-4666-1

Printed through Dai Nippon Printing Co., Ltd. in Korea
10 9 8 7 6 5 4 3 2 1

The paper used in this publication meets the minimum requirements of the American National Standard for Information Sciences—Permanence of Paper for Printed Library Materials, ANSI Z39.48-1992.

Harry N. Abrams, Inc.
100 Fifth Avenue
New York, N.Y. 10011
www.abramsbooks.com

Abrams is a subsidiary of